OTHER BOOKS BY THE SAME AUTHOR

The Catholic Milieu

Foundations of a Catholic Political Order

Christendom and the West: Essays on Culture, Society and History

From Christendom to Americanism and Beyond

An Economics of Justice and Charity: Catholic Social Teaching, Its Development and Contemporary Relevance

Louis Cardinal Billot, *Liberalism: A Critique of Its Basic Principles and Its Various Forms* (translator)

The Glory of the Cosmos: A Catholic Approach to the Natural World (editor)

Theology: Mythos or Logos? A Dialogue on Faith, Reason, and History (co-authored with John Médaille)

Seeing the World with Catholic Eyes

Seeing the World with Catholic Eyes

A CONVERSATION WITH
THOMAS STORCK

AROUCA PRESS

Copyright © Arouca Press 2021
Copyright © Thomas Storck 2021

All rights reserved:
No part of this book may be reproduced or transmitted,
in any form or by any means, without permission

ISBN: 978-1-989905-62-3 (pbk)
ISBN: 978-1-989905-63-0 (hardcover)

Arouca Press
PO Box 55003
Bridgeport PO
Waterloo, ON N2J3G0
Canada
www.aroucapress.com
Send inquiries to info@aroucapress.com

Disce ut semper victurus, vive ut cras moriturus.
— St. Edmund of Abington

CONTENTS

Publisher's Preface   xiii

1 Life & Intellectual Background   1
   Childhood—Importance of father's relationship to religion—Intellectual framework—C.S. Lewis—Aristotle—St. Thomas Aquinas—Richard Tawney's Religion and the Rise of Capitalism—Medieval Catholic Church—Counter-culture—Platonic thought in American society—Disordered sexuality as reaction to Platonism—Lack of unity among academic disciplines—'The Historical Point of View'—Neglect of older works—Pre-Socratics—Nominalism—St. Thomas follows Aristotle—Modern thought as nominalist—Immanuel Kant—Morality inherent in being—Philosophy as ancilla theologiae—*Thomism helps us think clearly—Thomism as the standard—Reaction to Thomism—Thomism must be applied to life—The Faith embodied in society (Middle Ages)—Chronological snobbery (analysis by C.S. Lewis)—Mathematics and Science as liberal arts—*Caelum et Terra *(involvement in this journal)—Intentional Catholic communities—Catholic intellectual revival of the twentieth century—Catholic attitude towards the natural world*

2 The Church   35
   Second Vatican Council—Hermeneutic of continuity—Gaudium et Spes—Growth of the Church in the United States—Price of the prosperity of the Church in the United States—Privatization of religion—Integralism—The role of the State in

legislating morality—First Amendment—Secularism as a religion—Religious liberty—Concept of a Catholic State—Brief view of John Paul II's pontificate—Kantian influence—Nominalism—Assisi meeting—Pope Francis—Amoris Laetitia—Laudato Si'—Abu Dhabi—Amazon Synod (Pachamama)—*Catholic teaching on the environment—Misuse of technology—Esotericism—Perennialism—Indifferentism—*Dignitatis Humanae—*Schemata of Vatican II*

3 Catholic Social Teaching 51

Left/right dichotomy—'Catholic' Americanism—Pius XI (encyclicals, Ubi Arcano, Quadragesimo Anno, Divini Redemptoris*)—Economic justice—Intelligent intervention in economic matters—Benedict XVI (encyclical,* Caritas in Veritate*)—Common good—John XXIII (encyclical,* Mater et Magister*)—Libertarian objection to the common good—Leo XIII (encyclical,* Immortale Dei*)—Economic models—Austrian school—Ludwig von Mises—Libertarianism—Paul VI (encyclical,* Octogesima Adveniens*)—John Paul II (encyclicals,* Laborem Exercens, Centesimus Annus*)—Economy not independent from morality—Definition of distributism (contrast to capitalism)—Economic activity oriented towards its proper end—Practical applications of distributism—Distributism does not restrict legitimate economic freedom—Fr. Heinrich Pesch (alternative model of just economic framework)—Rise of capitalism—Examples of economic practices prohibited in the Middle Ages (e.g., forestalling, usury)—Guilds—Definition of capitalism—Critique of capitalism—Separation of ownership and work—Hilaire Belloc—Different forms of capitalism (e.g., German system of co-*

Contents

determination)—Unions—Minimum wage—Radical change to our socio-economic system needed—Divisions among Catholics—Political action needed—Reasons for Catholic social teaching being buried—Dorothy Day and Peter Maurin—Subsidiarity

4 Liberalism   87

Definition of—American liberalism—Conservatism—Temporary alliances—Catholic view of Liberty—Leo XIII (encyclical, Libertas*)—Natural liberty—Political liberty—Debate on the success/failure of liberalism within society—John Locke*

5 Politics   97

Catholic involvement in politics—American Solidarity Party—Voting—Catholic media—Catholic/Protestant alliances—Right-to-life movement—Abortion—Homosexuality—Division of political opinions (chart of David Nolan)

6 Americanism   107

Leo XIII (Apostolic Letter, Testem Benevolentiae*)—Active virtues—Declaration of Independence—Dr. Benjamin Rush—American character—American exceptionalism—America as an 'idea'—American messianism—Patriotism*

7 Culture   113

Role of culture—Definition of—Belloc, 'Catholicism as a general culture'—Difference between Catholic and Protestant cultures—Examples of differences—Christopher Dawson on America—Individualism as an American trait

8   Living as Catholics in the Modern World   119
    Immigration to the United States—What is modernity?—Nominalism—Protestantism—French Revolution—Rod Dreher (Benedict Option)—Separation of God from reason—Role of mass media in shaping minds—Post-Protestant secularism—Christopher Dawson on the 'American religion'—Our duty to convert American culture—Why Catholics in the United States did not challenge the prevailing culture—Difficulty in converting non-Catholics—Keeping Catholics Catholic—how to resist despair—What we must do to keep a Catholic vision of life—Importance of reading good books (e.g., list of books)—Keeping out of ignorance—Maintaining a liberal education—Forming one's mind—Ontological evil precedes moral evil—Duty to understand modern errors—We must read widely

Guide to My Works:
Themes and Recommendations   137

PUBLISHER'S PREFACE

The thought of writing a preface for a book by Thomas Storck would have seemed incomprehensible but what a privilege and honor it has been to make a small contribution to his new book! I have known about his work for twenty years and always viewed him as an example of a serious Catholic thinker whose works cannot be easily pigeon-holed.

My first contact with Thomas Storck began in early 2019 when I took up the courage to ask if he was interested in working on a revised translation of Louis Cardinal Billot's Latin treatise on liberalism which itself was taken from the larger work, *De Ecclesia*. To my surprise he agreed to work on the revised translation since the original English translation was nearly unreadable given its slavish adherence to the Latin. He also provided an excellent introduction which situated Billot's analysis of liberalism within the American context.

We continued a correspondence and he was always generous in answering my questions on Catholic social teaching and other issues which I have always found interesting. He subsequently approached me last year and asked if Arouca Press would publish a book which he edited on the Catholic approach to the natural world. This appeared at the end of last year with the title, *The Glory of the Cosmos: A Catholic Approach to the Natural World*.

What I have always found refreshing and stimulating in Thomas Storck's works is his ability to write intelligently on so many topics. In this sense, Thomas Storck is a *universal* thinker who has been able to apply the Faith in a multi-disciplinary manner to contemporary problems. The intellectual—a word bandied about so easily—is at home in *many* fields for he does not compartmentalize his thought and can take a comprehensive view of reality. "Intellectuality admits of no compartments,"[1] says Sertillanges, and so it is that Storck's works rise above the narrow thinking of the specialists and, as a consequence, provide so much delight for the mind.

Rooted in the thought of St. Thomas Aquinas and the Church's rich intellectual tradition, the brilliance of C. S. Lewis, and other wise men (as you will read from the book you hold in your hands), Thomas Storck takes seriously the history of ideas. This is perhaps one of the main reasons why I have been so impressed with his work. What good is it to store so much theoretical knowledge without making connections with the real world—the world you and I have to slug our way through?

The idea for this book came about in an organic fashion. I originally thought of asking Mr. Storck if I could do an online interview with him. We soon realized that with a bit of a push we could develop this into a book.

The questions in *Seeing the World with Catholic Eyes* are meant to elicit provocative answers. The book begins with an exploration of his early life and intellectual background. What were the factors that helped shape his life as a public intellectual? Thomas Storck then answers questions related to the Church and some of the controversies that are being discussed today. Then—in the largest section of the book—he answers questions on Catholic social teaching. This is the theme that has most fascinated me because I would argue that one of the errors many Catholics have accepted today is the idea that the Church exists *solely* for an ethereal goal. The Church exists to lead people to heaven but the day-to-day workings of "real life"—so they argue—are best left to the certified "experts" who alone can provide the principles to ensure a successful life. Thomas Storck views the Church and

---

[1] A. D. Sertillanges, *The Intellectual Life*, (Westminster, MD: Newman, 1946), p. 170

her robust social teachings as *central* to helping Catholics create an environment where justice and charity can operate harmoniously. His thinking on distributism — an economic theory easily misunderstood — shows that the goal is ultimately that economic activity be oriented toward fulfilling "our needs and reasonable desires" and as such is in line with Catholic social teaching. It would be worth quoting from his book, *An Economics of Justice and Charity*:

> ...just as Catholics should look to the Church when forming their consciences about their conduct as individuals or within their families, so they should look to her when forming their consciences regarding their *social or economic or political conduct*. [my emphasis] (p. 103)

He continues in this series of question and answer by commenting on the nature of liberalism, which for the past several years has been the object of intense debate among many scholars and political commentators. He addresses specific political questions such as Catholic involvement in politics, and the division of political opinions which are sure to provide much source for reflection.

The other sections include a fascinating look into the nature of Americanism which has been a source of so much confusion because of the role the United States has played on the world stage and which has affected how Catholics in the United States view the Church's mission. The United States in many respects represents not so much a nation but an idea which divinizes its political framework. Read his answers!

He then goes on to answer some questions in relation to culture and how it manifests itself within a Catholicism practiced in the United States. The next section deals with questions related to Catholic living in the modern world, a world which is hostile to a Catholic ethos. The last section consists of a guide to his works where we see how his views "on the intersection between Catholic faith and life in this world" are given concrete form.

The tendency in modern religious discourse—as far as I see it—is towards the sound-byte, the superficial, and an almost total inability to have a meaningful discussion. In what we hope will be a compelling book, you are presented with a mind that has thought, and thought deeply upon the Catholic faith and *all* the ways it *must* animate our lives. We think the title is apt because it is truly an attempt to "see the world through Catholic eyes." Reflect upon his words. They might shake you a bit but maybe we haven't been shaken enough. The world won't be won over to Christ by half-heartedness and indifference.

1
Life & Intellectual Background

Could you tell us a little about your life growing up?

I guess in many ways my childhood was not untypical of the baby boom generation. My mother stayed home caring for our family and household, my father worked outside the home. This was the pattern for everyone I knew at that time. I remember our home life as placid. For a time my mother's parents lived with us.

In other ways, however, I think it was very different. My father was not a conformist, and although for the most part he didn't do much to call attention to himself, inwardly or mentally he thought for himself. I remember at the height of the cold war he used to listen to Radio Moscow on his short wave radio. Not that he was a Communist, in fact, he was a registered Republican for years, but of the Nelson Rockefeller kind of Republican. But he never simply allowed his thinking to be determined by someone else's ideology or by popular trends of thought. Although as with most Americans I think his ideas shifted considerably over the course of the last third of the last century, they did not simply shift in lockstep with current notions, however widespread. I suppose one would have to call him a liberal (in the American sense of the term), but he was not a typical liberal, and even late in life supported the death penalty, for example.

On religion, in particular, his thinking was very atypical of the average American of this era, that is, the 1950s and early 60s. Although our family was pretty regular in attending church while I was growing up, finally ending up in the Episcopal Church when I was about ten years old, my father did not really believe in God, at least not in any God that Christians or even theists do. Perhaps he could have been called an atheist, though he did not use that term for himself, perhaps a pantheist, for he liked to say he believed in a non-personal god. I remember once he said to me that perhaps $E=MC^2$ was god! But he very much believed in the social value of religion and church-going, and he liked to discuss religion. He had a large personal library and the religion section was one of the biggest parts of it. My father did not think that religion was something of no importance or something that husbands should leave to their wives, as I think many American men of that era did. He definitely set the religious tone for the family, and, paradoxically, even though he was an unbeliever, I think that this was very good for my intellectual and ultimately for my religious development, for my becoming, at first a believing Episcopalian, and later a Catholic. I grew up knowing that religion was something important, something worth discussing and having ideas about. So in a sense, it was an easy transition when I became a believer. I already realized religion was important; now I also realized that it could be true.

I recently came across an article, originally published in *Touchstone* in 2003, about the importance of fathers and churchgoing.[1] Although I'm sure he is speaking of fathers who actually believe the religion that they practice, I think what he says has application to the case of my father as well.

> In short, if a father does not go to church, no matter how faithful his wife's devotions, only one child in 50 will become a regular worshipper. If a father does go regularly, regardless of the practice of the mother, between two-thirds and three-quarters of their children will become

---

[1] Robbie Low, "The Truth About Men & Church," *Touchstone*, June 2003.

churchgoers (regular and irregular). If a father goes but irregularly to church, regardless of his wife's devotion, between a half and two-thirds of their offspring will find themselves coming to church regularly or occasionally.

A non-practicing mother with a regular father will see a minimum of two-thirds of her children ending up at church. In contrast, a non-practicing father with a regular mother will see two-thirds of his children never darken the church door. If his wife is similarly negligent that figure rises to 80 percent!...

A mother's role will always remain primary in terms of intimacy, care, and nurture. (The toughest man may well sport a tattoo dedicated to the love of his mother, without the slightest embarrassment or sentimentality). No father can replace that relationship. But it is equally true that when a child begins to move into that period of differentiation from home and engagement with the world "out there," he (and she) looks increasingly to the father for his role model. Where the father is indifferent, inadequate, or just plain absent, that task of differentiation and engagement is much harder. When children see that church is a "women and children" thing, they will respond accordingly — by not going to church, or going much less.

Curiously, both adult women as well as men will conclude subconsciously that Dad's absence indicates that going to church is not really a "grown-up" activity. In terms of commitment, a mother's role may be to encourage and confirm, but it is not primary to her adult offspring's decision. Mothers' choices have dramatically less effect upon children than their fathers', and without him she has little effect on the primary lifestyle choices her offspring make in their religious observances.

American culture, even when it has a religious veneer, as it did in the supposed religious revival that took place after World War II, has usually not had much intellectual interest in what it allegedly believes, not much interest in doctrine as such. You'll recall that the big debate over prayer in public schools, which was coming to a head in the early 1960s, was concerned with a prayer mandated by the state of New York that could be acceptable to nearly any theist, "Almighty God, we acknowledge our dependence upon Thee, and we beg Thy blessings upon us, our parents, our teachers and our country." Even in my high school years in the late 60s we had a moment of silent prayer as part of the announcements broadcast over the loudspeaker every morning in which we were exhorted to pray "each in his own words, each in his own way." Such vapid religion, it seems to me, is calculated to make students think that religion is merely a formality, certainly not something worth serious intellectual engagement, perhaps little different from the formal religion of late pagan antiquity which had become a merely civic observance.

So as you can see, my father had considerable influence on me, though not in the way one might have expected, or indeed in the way he expected. He was not happy about my becoming a believing Christian, though he didn't make much of a fuss about it. Having known so many from my generation whose families attended church regularly and outwardly professed belief, but for whom religious faith had little real meaning or substance, I am grateful to my father for my having grown up in a family that, although certainly unorthodox as regards religion, treated it as a matter of serious intellectual concern.

Life & Intellectual Background

What influenced you in developing your particular intellectual framework?

Though I always liked reading, and read a great deal of history from at least the upper elementary grades, it was only in my last two or three years in high school that I began to develop something that could reasonably be called an intellectual framework. In the summer before my junior year, that is, in the summer of 1967, I discovered C. S. Lewis, the Anglican writer who has been so influential for so many. I have described elsewhere how he, along with other authors, particularly G. K. Chesterton, helped lead me over the next six to eight months from an immature atheism to theism, and then to baptism in the Episcopal Church the next summer. About ten years later I entered the Catholic Church, the final stage of my journey.[2]

But Lewis did more than simply help me to embrace a Christian faith. He shaped my thinking in important ways, introducing me to the concept of natural law, for example, and to other classical intellectual concepts and ideas. Above all, that of a respect for reason and the obligation to adhere to a reasoned proof, regardless of one's feelings or what the contemporary intellectual atmosphere might be. I think *The Screwtape Letters* was the first book of Lewis' that I read, and I remember being very impressed when I read in the opening paragraph.

> I note what you say about guiding your patient's reading and taking care that he sees a good deal

---

[2] I have written about my conversion more than once. One version (as originally published in *New Oxford Review*) is available on the thomasstorck.org website. Others can be found in Marcus Grodi, ed., *Journeys Home 2* (Zanesville, Ohio: CHResources, 2014), pp. 141–154, and Dale Ahlquist, ed., *My Name is Lazarus* (Charlotte, N. C.: ACS Books, 2018), pp. 259–266. Also available is Marcus Grodi's interview of me about my conversion on the Coming Home Network website.

of his materialist friend. But are you not being a trifle *naïf*? It sounds as if you supposed that *argument* was the way to keep him out of the Enemy's clutches. That might have been so if he had lived a few centuries earlier. At that time the humans still knew pretty well when a thing was proved and when it was not; and if it was proved they really believed it. They still connected thinking with doing and were prepared to alter their way of life as the result of a chain of reasoning.

That made a big impression on me, the idea of adhering to rational proof, even of altering one's way of life as the result of a chain of reasoning. Lewis fixed in me the notion that regardless of what is popular or in fashion, regardless of how one feels, one has to adhere to what has been proven, to a truth that exists outside oneself. We must conform, as much as we can, with God's help to be sure, to reality as it exists. We cannot make up our own reality. This was perhaps the most important thing I learned from reading Lewis, and something I've tried to adhere to in my own life.

Thus when I entered college in the fall of 1969, I already had some principles which served as a rudimentary but essentially correct intellectual framework. This stood me in good stead during the next four years when very few of my professors were Christians, despite the fact that the college I was attending, Kenyon College in Ohio, was formally affiliated with the Episcopal Church. In fact, the atmosphere was almost entirely secular. But Lewis, and to a lesser extent, G. K. Chesterton, had armed me in advance, as it were, so that I recognized as shallow the arguments and attitudes that might otherwise have undermined my Christian faith

This early training from C. S. Lewis received its capstone, so to speak, when I studied Aristotle in college. He supplied the real foundations, the explicit metaphysical foundations, for the outlook that I had acquired from Lewis. Although I did read some St. Thomas in college, I read much more Aristotle, and it was chiefly via Aristotle that I later came to Thomism, in the sense that I gradually discovered, especially after I became a Catholic, how Thomas offered a more complete and coherent formulation of what is essentially an Aristotelian framework. So though Aquinas certainly had other intellectual influences besides Aristotle, Plato and Augustine, for example, it appears to me that those who would unduly downplay the fundamentally Aristotelian atmosphere of Aquinas are guilty of ignoring the forest for the trees, doing things like counting the number of references Thomas makes to any particular thinker, as if that were a good method of ascertaining someone's intellectual framework.[3]

I should also mention some of the literature courses I took, especially one on Chaucer and Middle English literature. Here the instructor was a believing Anglican, Gerrit Roelofs, and not at all shy about illustrating his lectures with Christian insights, especially about how classical Christian themes were embodied in our readings. This, of course, was easy to do with Chaucer, but it helped me to see how abstract points from theology or philosophy could be instantiated in concrete literary or cultural examples or practices.

I took most of the courses I could on ancient and medieval thought, and in fact I was focused so exclusively on earlier writers, that I neglected nearly all courses on modern literature, and when it came time to take my final comprehensive exams I was rather unprepared as regarded more recent authors and had to retake the exams at the end of the summer!

But there was another important part of my intellectual formation. Even before having any interest in Christianity I

---

[3] For example, see Mark Jordan, "The Alleged Aristotelianism of Thomas Aquinas," Toronto: PIMS, c. 1992.

had been interested in politics, and involved in small ways in what we would call liberal political activity for state and local races. But my political opinions were not based on much of a reasoned foundation, mostly taken without much reflection from my father. Some time during my junior or senior year in high school, about the same time as I was reading Lewis and Chesterton, I chanced upon Richard Tawney's *Religion and the Rise of Capitalism* at a bookstore.

I bought it knowing nothing about the author or the book, mostly (if I remember rightly) because it had this interesting picture on the cover of a stock ticker machine with a stained glass covering. But I read it and discovered that the medieval Catholic Church had a robust doctrine of economic morality, a doctrine which by and large fit with my own half-formed political and economic views. After reading Tawney I still knew nothing about the post-medieval history of that teaching, such as the modern papal social encyclicals, but Tawney began to give my socio-political opinions some grounding in reasoned Catholic thought and tradition. Naturally this went hand in hand with my newly developing Christian faith.

A third, somewhat surprising, source for my intellectual framework, was the counterculture of the 1960s. There was much that was bad in that movement, much hedonism and disordered sensuality, much rejection of reason—and without question it has generally been the negative aspects

Life & Intellectual Background

of this movement which have had such a sad and lasting influence on American culture. For most people it was, or soon became, simply an excuse to do whatever one felt like doing. But despite this, it contained a critique of materialism that resonated with my nascent Christian faith. Another of my Kenyon professors, Harry Clor, made this point in an interesting discussion about radical and countercultural critiques of American society.

> American society is said to be devoted to low, dull, and unexciting goals [and] this mediocrity is attributed to commercialism, a commercialism that produces an acquisitive, comfort-seeking, security-minded, and, hence, uninteresting way of life.
>
> This description of American life is no doubt exaggerated and oversimplified. But it is difficult, as well as unwise, to avoid the acknowledgement that there are some elements of truth in this description. In the United States a remarkable amount of attention is given to the accumulation and consumption of commodities. And we do not seem to mind being called a "consumer society." It does appear to be the case that for most Americans the pursuit of happiness has come to mean, in large measure, the attainment of economic security and the continual multiplication of the means for personal comfort and enjoyment.[4]

Such a critique of mere comfort and material goods, such as might be found in the Port Huron Statement or other New Left writings, could just as easily have been found in

---

4 Harry M. Clor, "American Democracy and the Challenge of Radical Democracy" in *How Democratic is America?*, edited by Robert A. Goldwin. (Chicago: Rand-McNally, 1969, 1973 printing) p. 105.

ancient pagan philosophers and thinkers, as well as Christian authors, both classical and contemporary. The Protestant writer, Francis Schaeffer wrote of this era:

> It became obvious to students in the early sixties that we were living in a post-Christian world. As students in Berkeley shouted in 1964, we are living in a plastic culture. The beat generation before them had been saying that, and now an entire student generation had become convinced of it. Students would return home from the university and ask their parents questions and would get only superficial answers: You must work like mad to get into the university. Why? So you can make money. But why should I want to make money? So you can send your children to the university. All too often personal peace and affluence were the only values that these young people saw in their parents, and they rightly were turned off.
>
> Christians should have been glad for what these students were saying. In fact, they should have been saying it themselves, for these young people had put their finger on the situation as it really was.[5]

In addition, there were two other related and fundamentally sound points that the counterculture made. First, an (inchoate and by no means well understood) appeal to nature as an ethical norm. Popular moral discourse, such as there was, at the end of the 1950s and beginning of the 60s tended to see all moral norms as simply societal conventions and did not distinguish well or at all between true ethical norms

---

5 Francis A. Schaeffer, *The New Superspirituality* (Downers Grove, Ill.: Inter-Varsity, 1972), p. 3.

and mere cultural practices. For example, there might be as much animosity toward a man having a beard as toward a real sin, such as adultery. So the appeal to ethical norms that were based on human nature made by the counterculture at its best was in itself a good thing. Related to this was the claim that the body was not being given sufficient recognition, and simply subordinated to the mind. Francis Schaeffer again, speaking of Protestant Evangelicalism:

> [Evangelical Christianity] had become infused with a large dose of Platonic thought. This Platonism showed itself in various ways. Perhaps the first way was in the attitude which many evangelicals had taken toward the body. The whole area of sex became taboo. You couldn't talk about this and you couldn't talk about that.... Because Platonism frowned on the body, the body was suspect, only the soul was good.[6]

What Schaeffer says here about Evangelicals was true in large measure for American society as a whole. Thus the attention on the part of the counterculture to nature and to the body was based on healthy instincts, by and large, but it was confused and lacked any philosophical understanding of what is even meant by nature or the natural. And the lack of intellectual underpinnings, and hence the inconsistencies and contradictions, that this confused recognition suffered from, showed itself immediately in two ways. First, the embrace of sexual freedom depended on widespread use of contraceptives as well as the availability of abortion, since the natural link between sexual activity and procreation was inconvenient for those seeking simply sexual pleasure. So in an ironic manner, those who claimed to want to live

---

6 *Ibid.*, p. 13.

naturally became dependent on contraceptives, on the very products of the chemical industry they otherwise scorned. In a sense they had made their own the advertising slogan of the time — *better living through chemistry*.

Secondly, very soon homosexual desires began to be put on the same level as the natural attraction of the two sexes toward each other. With no grasp of what it means to appeal to human nature as an ethical norm, our feelings and desires, whatever felt good, were labeled as natural. Natural became simply a synonym for 'whatever feels good,' or 'whatever one is inclined to do.' Of course this very faulty understanding of what is meant by *nature* was the result of generations of bad philosophical teaching.

Today things are even worse, since we have a situation in which many embrace the idea that our natural bodies are in effect so much worthless stuff, to be mutilated and chemically stunted at the behest of our minds, if one happens to feel that he is "imprisoned" in the wrong type of body, the wrong sex. This is Platonism on steroids. Or better, it is Cartesianism, Descartes's teaching that human beings are simply our minds and that our bodies are so much extended dead matter.

It seems both sad and highly ironic to me to look back fifty years to when people were claiming that they wanted to live more naturally, to give the body its due, and then to see what has happened in the meantime, with the body treated simply as an insignificant mass of matter to be manipulated at the behest of the mind.

Your intellectual activity has been mostly outside of academia. Has this created any difficulties for you? How do you see the work of a non-academic intellectual?

That is true, my total teaching experience in higher education is about the equivalent of a year and a half or two

Life & Intellectual Background

years full-time teaching. Not very much, to be sure. But this fact has not been something altogether negative, I think. My intellectual interests have always been broad, hard to pigeon hole into the academic departments into which contemporary higher education, and perforce, much of contemporary intellectual life, is divided. The boundaries of many of those fields are in fact artificial, merely conventional, and the most important questions naturally cross such disciplinary boundaries, and need to be treated using the intellectual approach of more than one discipline. Many of the modern academic fields, especially in the social sciences, originated as subdivisions of philosophy, but have since become detached from their parent subject and now regard themselves as independent areas of knowledge. But most of the time they deal with questions that have philosophical implications; they involve, for example, questions of political philosophy or of ethics, questions about what is the best life for mankind, the best way to live, to design cities. Questions about technology necessarily also have profound ethical implications, and so on. Most of these likewise have theological implications. So I think that the fact that I have worked outside of academia has made it easier for me to approach intellectual questions from whatever angle is appropriate, regardless of academic specialty and without having to worry about the canons of any particular discipline or the requirements of publishing that academia imposes.

The specialization and overspecialization that characterizes contemporary intellectual life is not heathy, and is in part responsible for its inward focus. For example, so many philosophical articles and dissertations do not deal directly with a philosophical question, but are a discussion of philosopher X's influence on philosopher Y, really an example of the history of philosophy rather than of philosophy itself. Now I would be the first to admit that such careful consideration of the history of philosophical thought is helpful, indeed necessary, for clarifying our knowledge of past thinkers. But it's not healthy that it has taken over such large swathes of intellectual life and turned people's attention away from dealing with actual philosophical questions.

This tendency to concentrate on what philosophers of the past thought or wrote, instead of on actual philosophical questions, does not simply divert our attention from philosophical problems, it paradoxically makes us less liable to regard older philosophers as thinkers who need to be taken seriously as sources of ideas. C. S. Lewis raises this point in *The Screwtape Letters*, speaking of the historical point of view.

> Only the learned read old books and we have now so dealt with the learned that they are of all men the least likely to acquire wisdom by doing so. We have done this by inculcating The Historical Point of View. The Historical Point of View, put briefly, means that when a learned man is presented with any statement in an ancient author, the one question he never asks is whether it is true. He asks who influenced the ancient writer, and how far the statement is consistent with what he said in other books, and what phase in the writer's development, or in the general history of thought, it illustrates, and how it affected later writers, and how often it has been misunderstood (specially by the learned man's own colleagues) and what the general course of criticism on it has been for the last ten years, and what is the "present state of the question". To regard the ancient writer as a possible source of knowledge—to anticipate that what he said could possibly modify your thoughts or your behaviour—this would be rejected as unutterably simple-minded. (Letter 27)

This is related to the tendency to regard the latest scholarship as definitive and as naturally displacing earlier works, instead of evaluating both impartially. I think this is especially true for historians, and indeed historical knowledge does grow. But every historian writes from a particular viewpoint, very often reflecting the viewpoint that is current in academia at the time. And these viewpoints not only change, but can change for the better or the worse. Of course, I'm speaking here in generalizations, but I think I'm not entirely wrong in saying this. My point here is not that we should ignore recent work but that there are many older texts very worthy of our continued esteem and use. These should not be considered as somehow "superseded," merely because they are old.

With regard to the second part of your question, about the work of the non-academic intellectual, the equating of intellectual work with academic work has likewise not been healthy for intellectual life, in my opinion. It's interesting that the noted book by the French Dominican, Fr. Antonin Sertillanges, *The Intellectual Life*, does not assume that someone engaged in the intellectual life must be an academic, indeed, as I recall, he doesn't even mention academia or teaching at all, but only study and writing. And if we look at significant intellectual figures from the past, even from just the last century and a half, say, many of them were not academics, yet made important contributions to our understanding of ourselves and the world. Often these contributions were less abstruse but still significant. I think the assumption that there are only two levels of discourse, academic and popular, is wrong, for there is a large in-between field where often the most interesting work has occurred and is occurring. The standards of academic writing obviously can and do vary according to time and place, and the notion that nothing serious can be written that does not adhere to contemporary academic standards is quite wrong-headed, as I see it.

There is certainly a danger in being a generalist, the danger of superficiality. So as I see it, intellectual life always exists in a kind of tension between the specialist, with his accompanying tendency toward narrowness and ultimate irrelevance, and the generalist, with his accompanying tendency toward superficiality. Both can learn from each other. The specialist can learn to transcend the often artificial boundaries of his field, and the generalist should make use of specialized knowledge and research to better ground his conclusions.

You mentioned Thomism. Can you expand on why that particular philosophy is important for the intellectual health of the Church?

Good philosophy is crucial, crucial for sound thinking in general, and crucial for good theology in particular. When we look at the world around us we're confronted with a mass of particular things, happenings, changes, everything seeming to be in a flux. Things grow and decay, they are born and they die. How do we make sense of all this? Is all of this simply so many individual, changeable things? Are there any principles, anything at all, which we can hold on to, as it were, and which might provide a framework for making sense of all this flux? This question was what seems to have inspired the first philosophers in Greece, the effort to make sense of change. Thus with Thales we have his dictum, *All is water*. Water can freeze, can melt into a liquid, can even boil away into the air. Yet it somehow remains the same thing. Here is a crude attempt to provide a foundation for understanding the constant change which we see around us, birth, death, destruction, etc. Other pre-Socratic philosophers wrestled with this problem also, some going so far as to deny change altogether, others to deny any stability. Plato worked out an interesting solution to this with his doctrine of forms, but it was Aristotle finally, with his insight into substances and accidents, and thus substantial and accidental change, who found the correct answer to the question posed by Thales.

Now it might seem as if this is a relatively minor point in philosophy. But I don't think so. The nominalists who began to dominate philosophy from shortly after the death of St. Thomas essentially rejected Aristotle's (and Aquinas') understanding, and turned or returned to a radically individualist view of things. There are no universals, they are mere names (*nomina*) that we apply to things. And this had extremely deleterious effects on European intellectual life. It was the chief cause of the unraveling of the medieval synthesis and the rise of modern philosophy and modern thought in general.

Now I know that there is a great deal more to the philosophy (not to mention the theology) of St. Thomas than this, but as far as his philosophy is concerned — and I make no pretense of speaking as a theologian — I think this question of universals, and all that it implies about change, and about the related question of the one and the many, is one of the most fundamental questions in philosophy. On this question, as well as many others, such as the mind's ability to know reality, Thomas followed Aristotle, "whose fundamental principles," Etienne Gilson noted, "he [Thomas] certainly identified with those of natural reason itself."[7] As I said before, there is much talk of the Platonic influences on Thomas, via Augustine and others, and certainly these should be acknowledged and not denied or downplayed. But I find it interesting that at one place in the *Summa Theologiae* Thomas rejects an argument of Augustine's, commenting that

---

7   Etienne Gilson, *Reason and Revelation in the Middle Ages* (New York: Charles Scribner's, c. 1938, 1966), p. 79.

"For this manner of speaking is common among Platonists, with whose doctrines Augustine was imbued; and the lack of adverting to this has been to some an occasion of error."[8]

Modern thought in general has been nominalist, it has neglected form and paid almost exclusive attention to matter. This is obvious in empiricist thinkers, but also in those influenced by the mighty figure of Kant, for if you make ultimate reality—the noumenal world—something that the human mind cannot reach, then all we are left with, when all is said and done, is the world of discrete and individual things, the world of matter. But with form—and here I'm using the term somewhat loosely—we necessarily must deal with purpose and with good and evil. You'll find articles, for example, claiming that 95% of the DNA of humans and chimpanzees, or whatever primate it might be, are identical, and the implication is that therefore there's little or no significant difference between them and us. But this is to consider matter only as important, as if one could say that since the stones and bricks out of which a church could be built are mostly the same stones and bricks out of which a concentration camp could be built, therefore there is little or no difference between them. Not an exact comparison, perhaps, but I think it gets my point across. It's form, it's the purpose for which something is made and which is largely inherent in its formal makeup, that is important, not the matter out of which they were constructed.

Modern thought looks upon morality as something extra; that's why ethics is such a big problem in modern philosophy. But morality is inherent in being, and being and goodness are convertible, as transcendentals. As I wrote elsewhere,

---

8 "*Hic enim modus loquendi consuetus est apud Platonicos, quorum doctrinis imbutus fuit Augustinus; quo quidam non advertentes, ex verbis ejus sumpserunt occasionem errandi*" (II-II, q. 23, art. 2, ad. 1)

We say something is good when that thing is whole and functions according to its inborn or "built-in" purpose. We say that a car that runs well is a good car, an athlete that usually wins in his particular sport is a good athlete, and that a swift race horse is a good race horse. When a thing functions successfully according to its purpose, we call it good. But according to its purpose as manifested by its nature, or being, as a whole. For it is not enough that a car's engine works, if at the same time its roof leaks, its tires are bare, or its headlights are broken. Unless it works according to the whole range of its functioning, we hesitate to call it good.

This connection between goodness and right functioning is embedded in our language and thought. Perfect means the highest degree of goodness; it also means that something has been finished or completed. The word perfect is derived from Latin *perficere*, to complete, to perfect. The participle, *perfectus*, means simply something that is completed or accomplished. In other words, when something is perfect, it has been made or finished as it is supposed to be; it can act according to its function. It is good.

Now obviously we are not speaking in the first instance of moral good here. A wrecked car and a lame race horse are not morally bad. The kind of good that we first uncover when we look at the relationship between goodness and functioning is ontological good, the goodness of being. What connection, though, does this kind of good have with moral goodness?

Moral goodness is in fact a subset of ontological goodness, a part of ontological goodness applicable only to creatures with intellect and will. A race horse is not blamed if it loses a race, and a car is certainly not legitimately blamed if it breaks down. That's because, if either of these is not functioning according to the fullness of its nature, there is no free choice on its part to blame. This principle applies to many aspects of human beings. For instance, we are not blamed if we are blind or sick (assuming that we did nothing to bring about those conditions), for in these respects we are like the race horse. But there is another side to human actions. While we might say that human beings have a certain perfection if we are healthy and have the use of all our limbs and our five senses, what if someone is a glutton or is so suspicious and quarrelsome that he can hardly get along with anyone or is someone who never keeps a promise, and so on? These defects are ontological, to be sure, in that they are part of our total human functioning, but they are also moral because at least to some degree—and apart from cases of psychological pathologies—they depend upon our free choices and the habits that we form or allow to grow up in us. Moral goodness and badness are simply that part of ontological goodness or badness that is more or less subject to our free choice. And because our possession of intellect and will is what specifically distinguishes us from the other animals, who lack these endowments, the goodness or badness which depend upon our intellect and will mark out a human being as good or bad more clearly than any mere ontological deficits, deficits which have absolutely no moral aspect. Thus a bad man is not someone who is blind or lame, but someone who steals or cheats and so on.[9]

Both Evangelical Protestants, with their notion that morality is something imposed as merely positive law through the Bible, and those philosophers who can't figure out the connection between being and morality, are representative of this tendency. This understanding of morality as something extra, something added from the outside, and hence detached from the real business of living, is extremely common in the United States, certainly. But by making morality something that is detached from life, from being, from reality, in effect it is destroyed or at least rendered unimportant, almost effete. One can see this very well in discussions of warfare. Those who glory in being "realists" when it comes to war and foreign policy are rarely restrained by any ethical considerations—they just want to get the job done, as they see it, and if destroying entire cities or making war on a peaceful nation is necessary, then, it's just something that has to be done. We can't let something as ethereal as morality stand in the way of real life.

Another way in which Aquinas (and Aristotle) is so important is brought out in this remark of Josef Pieper that St. Thomas "was intrepidly affirming the whole of natural reality, not only with regard to objective existence, but also *within* man himself...."[10] Both philosophers wanted to give an account of reality, not straitjacket reality into a system the way many later thinkers endeavored to do. The great intellectual systems of modernity, beginning at

---

9 "An Approach to Natural Law," thejosias.com, July 25, 2018.
10 Josef Pieper, *Guide to Thomas Aquinas* (Notre Dame: University of Notre Dame, 1987), p. 121.

least with Descartes and lasting at least to Freud, based themselves on reality at one or a few points only, and subjected everything else to the logical working out of their systems. The attraction that their systems exercised came from whatever contact they had with reality, with their ability to explain some things, and from their intellectual coherence, but they failed because they attempted to explain everything with a few leading ideas. They were not content simply to describe the order and structure that actually exists, but created in large part imaginative attempts to impose something on the world around them. Chesterton put this is a colorful but apt way:

> Since the modern world began in the sixteenth century, nobody's system of philosophy has really corresponded to everybody's sense of reality: to what, if left to themselves, common men would call common sense. Each started with a paradox: a peculiar point of view demanding the sacrifice of what they would call a sane point of view. That is the one thing common to Hobbes and Hegel, to Kant and Bergson, to Berkeley and William James. A man had to believe something that no normal man would believe, if it were suddenly propounded to his simplicity; as that law is above right, or right is outside reason, or things are only as we think them, or everything is relative to a reality that is not there. The modern philosopher claims, like a sort of confidence man, that if once we will grant him this, the rest will be easy; he will straighten out the world, if once he is allowed to give this one twist to the mind.[11]

---

11 *St. Thomas Aquinas* in *The Collected Works of G. K. Chesterton*, vol. II (San Francisco: Ignatius, c. 1986), p. 514.

Life & Intellectual Background

When we consider philosophy in relation to theology, as *ancilla theologiae*, the handmaid of theology, we can likewise see the necessity of good philosophy. Consider the heresy of modernism, labeled by St. Pius X as the "synthesis of all heresies." It is at bottom a philosophical error, one heavily infected by philosophic idealism, by the idea that reality is closed to the human mind, that essentially we are limited to knowing concepts within our own intellects, that the real world is closed to us. Pretty obviously that has disastrous effects for theology. While it is true, and a point that St. Thomas fully accepts, that we cannot know God in his essence with our finite minds, nevertheless the Church teaches that we can know some things about God using our reason, in particular that he exists, as well as other important truths, such as the immortality of the soul, not to mention truths of the purely natural order.

Another characteristic of the mind imbued with a Thomistic sense is the tendency to think clearly, and hence to speak and write and act clearly. This was considered one of the hallmarks of Catholic thinking before the Council. I think that one of the reasons, probably the main reason, why since the Council so many statements, and even more, so many actions by Catholic prelates have conveyed an ambiguous message is the lack of a sound philosophy. It has been said that Thomism is the philosophy of common sense, and it often seems as if common sense is sorely lacking in today's Church.

If Thomism is important for the intellectual health of the Church, how do you evaluate the currents of thought in the contemporary Church?

Leo XIII, Pius X and their successors encouraged and even mandated the teaching of Thomism in Catholic educational institutions, especially seminaries. Sometimes it was taught in a dry and uninteresting manner, as something imposed by authority but not in itself of much interest or value. While some of the old philosophical or theological textbooks and manuals are valuable and well worth study today, others of them simply classify things with endless divisions and distinctions, and never bother to point out why all of this is important. As a result there was a kind of reaction against Thomism, and by the time of the Second Vatican Council many were happy to cast it off as old-fashioned and uncreative. This was a mistake, for Thomism, as an orderly philosophical account of reality, is actually the most exciting and interesting way of doing philosophy. The fact that it has been around for a long time is, of course, neither here nor there, for truth does not depend on the particular chronological era in which it is discovered or formulated. As a result of this turn away from Thomism, Catholic philosophy and theology began to base itself on a plethora of modern systems of thought, on Kant, on existentialism, and so on. I think this has had an extremely bad effect on Catholic thought and life, extending even to the everyday life of the Church. Although there has been a noticeable reaction back toward Thomism, in both academic and other intellectual circles, it appears that this has a long way to go before we take up where we left off in the early 1960s.

One of my concerns about Thomism, however—and this concern would have been valid even before the Council—is that the highest principles of metaphysics can be correctly taught and learned, and yet they remain hanging in the air, so to speak, that is, the principles of philosophy do not influence our everyday political, social or cultural attitudes or opinions or judgments. So it's possible to be able to enunciate all the correct formulas of logic or metaphysics, and yet as far as one's socio-political opinions go, be a thorough-going Americanist or Lockean. This is the fault, in great part, I think, of those who teach philosophy, for they apparently simply assume that their students will apply these abstract philosophical principles correctly and make the right deductions from them. But any acquaintance with current Catholic thought will reveal this this is not true. The older I get the more I think that people need not only to be told what are the right ideas or principles, but to have it pointed out to them what are the deductions which follow from these first principles, and also what ideas and principles are *not* right. For it amazes me how people can hold ideas or propositions that contradict what are supposedly their first principles and not realize that this presents, or should present, a problem or difficulty for them.

Is it right to identify Catholic philosophy so closely with one school of thought, or even with one philosopher or theologian, St. Thomas? Haven't Catholics worked fruitfully within many different philosophical schools? Shouldn't a Catholic thinker have freedom to use another philosophical or theological framework to explore reality provided there is no conflict with the Catholic Faith?

Although Pope Pius XI wrote in his 1923 encyclical *Studiorum Ducem* that "the Church has adopted [Thomas's] philosophy for her own" (no. 11), it would not be quite true to say that thereby other philosophers or theologians were ever entirely excluded. Jesuits, for example, held in high esteem their own philosophers, such as Suárez, and Franciscans likewise with John Duns Scotus. But the times when philosophical schools totally at variance with that of St. Thomas were in the ascendancy, e.g., during the seventeenth or eighteenth centuries when Descartes' philosophy exercised considerable influence in the Church, were generally not eras when Catholic thought was at its best. I would say that the period since the Second Vatican Council has been another such era, and the often erroneous philosophical foundations of so many Catholic thinkers of today are largely responsible for the errors and confusion and even for just the vagueness and insipidity of so much Catholic writing today at every level, as I just noted.

Given your mention of the "medieval Catholic Church," what actually can we learn from studying the Church in the Middle Ages? A typical reply you may get is that medieval men had an ignorant and unenlightened understanding of society, man, and God. Isn't the twenty first century the apotheosis of our knowledge of these three things?

The main thing of value we can see in the Middle Ages and the Church of the Middle Ages is a society in which the Catholic faith was incarnated, enculturated, made part of the very fabric of society. This is what Catholics should always aim for, because the Faith is not just a set of ideas or even a set of religious practices and rituals, but in addition it ought to transform all of our lives, all of society. As the Vatican II document, *Gaudium et Spes* puts it, it is the task of the laity "to see that the divine law is inscribed in the life of the earthly city" (no. 43). In the Middle Ages this was achieved, imperfectly, to be sure, but reasonably well, given this fallen world, and whether we study medieval thought at its highest level—theology and philosophy—or literature or architecture or economics, we will discover a society in which the truths of the Faith were expressed or embodied in society and its institutions.

The notion that medieval man was unenlightened, that we today are wiser than all those of the past—this is just chronological snobbery, as C. S. Lewis expressed it in his autobiography, *Surprised by Joy*.

> [Owen] Barfield never made me an Anthroposophist, but his counterattacks destroyed forever two elements in my own thought. In the first place he made short work of what I have called my "chronological snobbery," the uncritical acceptance of the intellectual climate common to our own age and the assumption that whatever has gone out of date is on that account discredited. You must find why it went out of date. Was it ever refuted (and if so by whom, where, and how conclusively) or did it merely die away as fashions do? If the latter, this tells us nothing about its truth or falsehood. From seeing this, one passes to the realization that our own age is also "a period," and certainly has, like all periods, its own characteristic illusions. They are likeliest to lurk in those widespread assumptions which are so ingrained in the age that no one dares to attack or feels it necessary to defend them.[12]

Because we know how to manipulate the natural world so effectively, we feel that we have real knowledge of that world and are so much smarter than our ancestors. To some extent we do have more knowledge, but not nearly so much as we think, and not usually on the most important matters. And in other areas, for example, philosophy, the medievals were way ahead of us.

And even with regard to the natural sciences, I have been impressed for some time by the thought of Thomas Kuhn and his seminal book, *The Structure of Scientific Revolutions*. Kuhn argued that scientists are always working within paradigms, mental structures that approximate the natural world around us, but that never completely accord with it. When a new

---

12 *Surprised By Joy* (New York: Harcourt, Brace, Jovanovich, c. 1955), pp. 207–208.

paradigm replaces an earlier one, for example, the Copernican view of planetary movement replacing the Ptolemaic, the new paradigm is not necessary any closer to reality than the old one, simply that it gets at certain things the old paradigm missed, but usually misses certain things the old paradigm got. Some have seen Kuhn's ideas as a kind of intellectual relativism, and insofar as they have been extended to philosophy or the social sciences, I think this is true. But he himself did not intend that they be applied outside of the natural sciences. And as a matter of fact, C. S. Lewis, in the Epilogue of his book, *The Discarded Image*, put forth ideas about scientific truth very similar to those of Kuhn. In any case, just because we know how to send astronauts to the moon hardly means we have more wisdom than our ancestors, medieval or otherwise.

The natural sciences are generally taught according to the reigning consensus, according to the current model or paradigm. And explicitly or implicitly it is assumed that their chief aim is the manipulation of the natural world, the power that Francis Bacon set forth as the end of knowledge. I simply assumed that that was their purpose and as a result did not have much interest in them. It was in large part my graduate studies at St. John's College in Santa Fe that allowed me to see how mathematics and the natural sciences could be approached in a liberal manner, i.e., as part of the liberal arts and not as mere techniques for the manipulation of nature, or as regards mathematics, as systems of symbolical manipulation with little or no reference to anything beyond, as they are taught nearly everywhere. Until then I had avoided as much as I could any mathematical or scientific studies, especially after an unfortunate experience in high school with the senior mathematics course. But at St. John's I discovered how these could be approached in a liberal or philosophic way, and how in doing so they were no longer mere techniques oriented toward technology and control of nature. At Kenyon as part of my requirements I had taken a course called Mathematical Concepts, popularly known as Poets' Math. Among other things we learned to manipulate infinite sets and supposedly proved that some infinite sets were larger than others, e.g., the real numbers larger than the integers. This made no sense to me — how could two infinites be of different sizes — but my attempt at dialog with the professor did not lead to much, as neither he nor I understood the real nature of the question. At St. John's I once mentioned this casually to a tutor who explained to me that the whole problem rested on the distinction Aristotle made between the potential and the actual infinite. Aristotle, of course, denied the latter, and I saw at once that the mathematics professor had simply *assumed* the existence of the actual infinite, and since I did not grasp the philosophic point at issue, I was not able to argue effectively or even bring up my real point of concern. The odd thing is that I had discussed my difficulties at the time with my philosophy professor at Kenyon, and though I know he was by no means ignorant of Aristotle, he never suggested the obvious way out of the difficulty.

In the 1990s you were involved with the journal Caelum et Terra. What was that journal and what was important about it?

Caelum et Terra, which existed from 1991 to 1996, was the brainchild of its editor, Daniel Nichols, who stated its purposes in an editorial in the first issue (summer 1991).

> We, the founders of this journal, are deeply dissatisfied with the current state of the Church... with the watered-down faith found in many of our parishes and schools as well as with the reaction, which seems to see the 1940s and '50s as the golden age of Catholicism. We are appalled, too,

by the domination of faith by politics, whether of the left or of the right....

What we hope for, ultimately, is nothing less than the transformation of society. We yearn to help build a culture which nurtures a more reflective life, which encourages heart and mind to open in contemplation of God and the sacramentality of creation, where justice and moral truth again inform the economic and political spheres.

Caelum et Terra's aims were ambitious and idealistic, and although there was talk of establishing intentional Catholic communities (including an article by me about how we might set one up), nothing came even of this, and obviously we did not manage to transform society. But I think the magazine did something very important, and this was to offer a model of faithful Catholicism, both as something conceptualized and as something lived, that was an alternative to both the conservative and liberal models of the Faith. At that time, in the early 90s, the conservative Catholic model had not yet assumed the dominating position, with its powerful network of institutions and publications, that it achieved during the latter part of the reign of John Paul II and of Benedict XVI. But it was beginning to do so. And for people looking around for a way to be Catholic this conservative model was and still is very attractive. It seemingly offers the traditional faith, traditional devotions, reverence toward the sacred, and so on. But it is partial at best, and at worst fraudulent. It is dominated more by a political than a theological vision, it is severely compromised on the nature of Catholic social teaching, and it is bound up with an idea of America almost as the Catholic promised land. In many ways it is a twenty-first century version of the old Americanism of Archbishop Ireland and Cardinal Gibbons, without even

Gibbons' saving grace of having prevented the condemnation of the Knights of Labor. But since liberal Catholicism offers at best a thin and insipid version of Catholicism, and at its worst has surrendered totally to contemporary secular culture, it is quite understandable why people turn to conservative Catholicism. So *Caelum et Terra* was important in offering people something concrete which avoided the errors and omissions of both the conservatives and the liberals.

Most people need some more concrete manifestation of an idea than simply reading about it in books and giving it mental assent. *Caelum et Terra* was important as an actually existing thing, a movement even, which sponsored gatherings where people could meet and exchange ideas, an actual manifestation of a Catholicism which was orthodox yet not conservative. If people are convinced that Catholicism is simply a way of baptizing conservative Americanist ideology, many will reject it. Sadly *Caelum et Terra* is gone now, and in its later purely online iterations toward the end was not able to avoid falling itself into the ideological trap the editors had so clearly discerned and avoided when it began.

Caelum et Terra reminds me of the early years of Integrity magazine (1946–1956), which offered a counter-vision to the one presented by many Catholic periodicals in the United States. It ultimately did not make much of a dent in how Catholics viewed the prevailing culture. Wouldn't it be a better approach to try to accommodate this environment rather than presenting such a sharp criticism? Isn't it better to work within rather than against the 'system' Catholic find themselves in to achieve a greater degree of success?

Here, it seems to me, the devil may lie in the details. It depends upon what we mean by an accommodation to the prevailing environment. Certainly when there are widely-held ideas that are not harmful to faith, then it might be a better counsel to go slowly and work on more important matters first. But it's also very easy to make fatal compromises and mistakenly believe that you can work within a system that is in fact undermining everything you're trying to achieve. And I think that in the case of bourgeois Americanism this *is* the case. If Catholics simply accept it and do not critique it, then we have short circuited all our apostolic efforts at the outset. If American culture merits a critique, and even a criticism, based on Catholic principles, we are doing nobody a favor if we refrain from such a critique and such criticism because of misplaced ideas of how to achieve success.

In what way do you think the Catholic Faith can inform each Catholic, whether laity or clergy, to view properly the world at-large?

Well, it seems obvious to me that if the Catholic faith is true, then it ought to show us how to look properly at the world, at all creation, at *everything*. Certainly the Church has not pronounced on everything, but very often we can, as it were, make deductions from what the Church *has* taught, to follow out the implications of these teachings for other matters. Here one very important thing is to learn from earlier Catholic writers, from St. Thomas, from the many excellent writers and thinkers of the Catholic intellectual revival of the late nineteenth and first half of the twentieth centuries. Writers such as Chesterton, Belloc, Christopher Dawson, Ronald Knox and so many others can serve as guides for us in almost every area of life and thought. They can help us to see Catholic teaching and Catholic attitudes made concrete, as it were. For it's unfortunately too easy to grasp Catholic principles on an abstract level, while our concrete socio-political, cultural, artistic opinions come from elsewhere, from our prejudices, from the intellectual atmosphere in which we were raised, and so on. The writers I've mentioned can help us to avoid a disconnect between the important abstract metaphysical principles and their application to concrete things in this world.

One obvious illustration of this is the cultivation of a Catholic attitude toward the natural world, the environment. Although recent pontiffs, especially Benedict XVI and Francis have spoken and written about this, prior to John Paul II there was little attention paid to that question in papal utterances. But important Catholic thinkers such as Romano Guardini and Christopher Dawson had set forth an attitude based on principles implicit in Catholic thought, but which had not been extensively discussed previously because mankind's adverse impact on the environment was not widely recognized until relatively recent times. The book I edited and which Arouca Press recently published, *The Glory of the Cosmos*, attempts a presentation of such a Catholic attitude toward the created world.

2
The Church

In 1925, Pope Pius XI issued his encyclical Quas Primas *on the Social Kingship of Christ. In what way is the Social Kingship of Christ related to Catholic social teaching? It has been argued that with the Second Vatican Council this concept has been relegated to one of a merely 'spiritual' doctrine with no connection with economic or political life. The various liturgical texts in the older Roman breviary for the feast of Christ the King expressed a robust sense of Christ's Kingship, but the liturgical reform significantly modified and muted this content. How do you explain these changes?*

It's possible to overemphasize differences between the teachings of the Second Vatican Council or post-conciliar teachings, with the previous utterances of the Magisterium. We should remember that the Council says that it is the task of the laity to "impress the divine law on the affairs of the earthly city" (*Gaudium et Spes*, no. 43). There is certainly a lot that was said and written during and since the Council that I regret or that I wish had been said differently. But if we hold that Jesus Christ continues to direct his Church, then I think we have to look at continuities, in fact, to make use of a hermeneutic of continuity, whenever that can reasonably be done. This is not some Pollyannaish approach, but simply one that recognizes both that the Holy Spirit continues to guide the Church and secondly, that documents produced as collective efforts, or in an official capacity — for example encyclicals — have different canons of interpretations from ordinary writings by individuals. In the latter it is perfectly proper, indeed necessary, to look for differences in outlook, and so on, to look for what is unique about the particular author or even the particular book. But in the former one is dealing with official utterances that have a kind of collective spirit or mind behind them. And the fact that the Holy Spirit grants them some level of guidance makes this even more the case. Of course, there are different levels of authority for different kinds of papal or ecclesiastical documents, and it is only to those of the highest authority that this approach fully applies. But I think it's a healthy approach to take in general for ecclesiastical documents, rather than immediately jump to the conclusion that there is some contradiction.

This is not to say that we can't recognize that, unfortunately, the Church, or rather, those who are ruling the Church, *are* often influenced by the intellectual climate that surrounds them. This seems painfully obvious today and frequently since the Council. But still, my first point remains, that we shouldn't overemphasize these differences, for the Church's voice is found not merely in her most recent utterances, but in what she has spoken throughout her history.

It would be difficult to argue against the material growth of the Catholic Church in the United States since the U. S. was founded. Doesn't this imply that the American 'system,' the political and philosophical foundation of the U. S., has been a wonderful environment within which the Church can operate?

No. In the first place, this question was directly addressed by Leo XIII in his encyclical, *Longinqua Oceani*, of January 1895, addressed to the American bishops. Pope Leo wrote (nos. 5 and 6),

> the prosperous condition of Catholicity must be ascribed, first indeed, to the virtue, the ability, and the prudence of the bishops and clergy; but in no slight measure also, to the faith and generosity of the Catholic laity.... But, moreover (a fact which

it gives pleasure to acknowledge), thanks are due to the equity of the laws which obtain in America and to the customs of the well-ordered Republic. For the Church amongst you, unopposed by the Constitution and government of your nation, fettered by no hostile legislation, protected against violence by the common laws and the impartiality of the tribunals, is free to live and act without hindrance. Yet, though all this is true, it would be very erroneous to draw the conclusion that in America is to be sought the type of the most desirable status of the Church, or that it would be universally lawful or expedient for State and Church to be, as in America, dissevered and divorced. The fact that Catholicity with you is in good condition, nay, is even enjoying a prosperous growth, is by all means to be attributed to the fecundity with which God has endowed His Church, in virtue of which unless men or circumstances interfere, she spontaneously expands and propagates herself; but she would bring forth more abundant fruits if, in addition to liberty, she enjoyed the favor of the laws and the patronage of the public authority.

The Church, Leo asserts, "would bring forth more abundant fruits if, in addition to liberty, she enjoyed the favor of the laws and the patronage of the public authority." We can be happy that, unlike in some European and Latin American countries where the Church went from enjoying the protection of the government to being hindered and even persecuted, the Church here did enjoy freedom to order her own affairs. But from the fact that freedom is better than persecution it does not follow that "the patronage of the public authority" would not confer great benefits on the

Church. The proof of this lies in our contemplation of Christendom, the great civilization in which Church and state worked together for the spiritual and temporal common good.

Moreover, the prosperity — rapidly vanishing, by the way — of the Church in the United States has come at a price, at the price of the privatizing of religion, the idea that the social order is essentially secular, or at least requires only a vague civil religion that differs little from deism. This unfortunate idea has infected the minds of most Catholics in the United States, and it is probably the chief effect of what you call the American system. This notion that dogmatic religion is essentially a private affair had done much to deform the minds of Catholics in the United States, and is partly responsible for their lack of enthusiasm for Catholic teaching on the political and social order.

What is Integralism? Is it practical? If so, does it offer any solutions to contemporary problems?

The website, *The Josias*, for which I have written, defines Integralism in this way:

> Catholic Integralism is a tradition of thought that rejects the liberal separation of politics from concern with the end of human life, holding that political rule must order man to his final goal. Since, however, man has both a temporal and an eternal end, integralism holds that there are two powers that rule him: a temporal power and a spiritual power. And since man's temporal end is subordinated to his eternal end, the temporal power must be subordinated to the spiritual power.

I think this gets at the heart of the matter, the classical and medieval view that politics was concerned with ultimate things. For a Catholic this means our eternal salvation. Of course, the political community and the Church do not exercise this concern in the same way. But the state must be about more than protection of property or of our rights, real or supposed. It must order man to virtue, and hence to eternal life.

Is this practical for today? That depends on what you mean. If you mean is there any real hope of such a regime being established today, I would certainly say No. But it's practical in the sense that it corresponds today as much as ever to the real human situation, to our human nature, to our nature as political and social beings, to our real needs, and to the teaching of the Church. Were we to have a genuine mass conversion to the Catholic faith, there is absolutely no reason why a government that adhered to intelligent integralist principles could not be established.

Isn't there a danger when the State concerns itself with religious matters? You often hear the State shouldn't legislate morality. The argument goes that this blurs the lines between political authority and ecclesiastical or religious authority.

There's a lot to unpack in your question. First, a state *always* legislates morality, always. It's inescapable. To have a law against theft or murder is to legislate morality, and to define theft in a certain way—e.g., to write the law so that deceiving consumers through misleading advertising is *not* theft—is obviously to take a stand on the moral question of what theft is or is not. Even not to have a law prohibiting or regulating some practice can be to take a stand, as it either says that the community does not regard the practice in question as wrong or at least as not violating the common good in any important way. So for moral matters I think it's clear—there is no way to avoid legislating on morality.

As to religion, that's a more complex question. Again, in a way no state can avoid taking a religious stance. The first clause of the First Amendment to the U. S. Constitution, "Congress shall make no law respecting an establishment of religion," effectively sets forth a religious policy just as much as would the explicit establishment of a state religion. For our First Amendment in effect says that religion is not a subject of official community recognition. It is a private matter. This seems obvious to most Americans, and was an obvious and convenient way of avoiding the religious strife that had plagued Europe for several centuries before our Constitution was written. But it is strange, really, that the body politic, which, as I just pointed out, unavoidably takes a stand on many moral matters, proclaims itself agnostic on a subject of the greatest interest and concern to mankind. If religion is important, if discovering the truths about God and our eternal destiny, is important, why should this be outside the official purview of the community organized as a *polis*?

There is a further aspect to this, though. Depending on what we mean by *religion*, does a secular state in fact establish liberalism or secularism as a religion? In practice, I think it necessarily does, for to exclude supernatural religion from official consideration by the community not only proclaims that it is not important, but it states that mankind's entire focus should be on the things of this world. Of course, any citizen is free to think otherwise, to live his life in light of the four last things, but, again, this is a purely private matter, something which the community as such judges to be of no significance. An analogy might help here. The public schools in the United States have long excluded religion, and never taught officially any form of dogmatic Christianity. It was said that if parents wanted to teach their children religion, then they were free to do so at home or in Sunday school, and so on. The school was not taking a stand *against* religion, and parents were free to say what they wanted about religion at home. In no way did this indicate an attitude one way or the other about the truth or importance of any religious tenets. But this was not really true. If the public schools, for example, had not taught mathematics, and had said, 'We're certainly not against mathematics, we allow parents to teach mathematics at home, should they choose to do so. We simply don't do it ourselves.' If schools had said something like that, it would have been clear that they didn't consider mathematics to be really important. If you omit teaching something, then you're saying that it's of little or no value, no matter how much you assert the freedom of parents to teach it at home. Similarly with the state and religion. If you ignore the subject, you are saying it's not important. Of course, in a religiously pluralistic society, there would need to be some accommodation to that fact. But to recognize the fact of pluralism and make concessions to it is not the same as to ignore the subject altogether and relegate it to the realm of private opinion.

When we speak of an "official religion" of the State, a typical modern response would be that it is better if the State did not endorse any one religion, otherwise it would cause unnecessary conflict in the body politic. How would you respond?

Well, I think the previous question suggests my answer. First, by officially ignoring religion, the state is still taking a stand of a sort. Secondly, although I recognize the fact that it would have been politically impossible for the United States at the time of the adoption of the Constitution to have a state religion, that doesn't mean that it had to go entirely to the opposite extreme and proclaim that the government has absolutely no concern with religion at all. There were other possibilities. In fact, it's an interesting thought, but perhaps if the half dozen or so state religious establishments that existed at the time had been more robust, both intellectually and politically, then this might have suggested a possible intermediate position. But those state establishments were clearly on their way out. I'm not aware of any important voices defending them on the fundamental ground that the community as such ought to concern itself with the most important matters that can concern mankind: our eternal destiny and what God requires of us in this world. Of course, this would have required that the state governments themselves were more robust, that they took advantage more skillfully of whatever possibilities were latent in the Constitution to assert their authority and power over against that of the federal government. That, however, would have been a huge task, for the trends were all in favor of the centralizing federal power.

The lack of recognition for religion at the official level has made it possible for American foreign policy to be amoral, and if anyone had qualms of conscience about that, those qualms must remain on the personal level. So if, for example, anyone in the military had refused to participate in the mass bombings during World War II, I think there's little doubt but that the authorities would have had no patience with the judgments of his conscience, and that he would have had to deal with them as a religious believer. But as a citizen, he was not to allow such qualms of conscience to interfere with his military duties. And in the religious liberty litigation at the Supreme Court level, questions of religious truth were not given serious consideration, but were dismissed as merely private affairs, matters of personal opinion. This has been a constant from the 1878 case of *Reynolds v. United States* to *Employment Division v. Smith* in 1990. Questions of religious liberty are always adjudicated according to secular principles, a point found in John Locke and taken over from his political philosophy.

Are there any models of a Catholic state which perhaps can teach us something about the way a State can be ordered properly?

From the conversion of the Emperor Constantine and the subsequent acceptance of Catholicism as the official religion of the Roman Empire all the way up till the twentieth century there were regimes which made the Catholic religion the official religion of the state or did so in effect. The variations of this system were immense, in some cases they involved the proscription of other religions, in other cases non-Catholics suffered some civil disabilities but not serious persecution, in others it was chiefly a symbolic recognition of the Church without much direct impact on society. In addition, as I said when speaking about the Middle Ages, social and cultural life as a whole, the economy, for example, was based on Christian principles during much of this time.

As to details, this is a huge subject, and a full answer would require historical scholarship beyond what I possess. For we have over a thousand years of a Catholic social order to look at if we want to learn how a Catholic political order can work and to evaluate better and worse ways of doing so. But a couple of books do exist which survey the situation in a more compact form. One is Fr. Edward Cahill's 1932 book, *The Framework of a Christian State*, still available today. Another is my own 1998 book, *Foundations of a Catholic Political Order*, which is also available. A free download of the latter book may be found on the website, thomasstorck.org

Pope John Paul II (1978–2005) presents a challenge for many Catholics. He was criticized by many heterodox priests and prelates for being too traditional (especially in regard to his upholding of Catholic teaching on sexual morality), yet he is also criticized by many for advancing heterodoxy, especially in terms of his approach to ecumenism. It doesn't seem like simplistic black and white answers are helpful in understanding his pontificate. How then can we accurately assess the long pontificate of John Paul II?

This is an interesting question but not an easy one to answer, at least for me. The contradictory tendencies you mention may well have something to do with his philosophical background, for in a very important way theology is dependent on philosophy. For instance, to use an extreme example, one who held to a strict Kantian notion that the real world, the so-called noumenal world, was beyond our ability to know and that our knowledge was limited to phenomena, could hardly agree with St. Paul who wrote in the first chapter of the epistle to the Romans that God's "invisible nature, namely, his eternal power and deity, has been clearly perceived in the things that have been made." Nominalism would be another example of a philosophical position that has serious theological implications. But in John Paul's case I do not know enough of his philosophy to speak to this question. But I agree that it is a concern, for some of his acts and statements do seem to indirectly undermine the foundations of the Faith. E.g., the Assisi gathering. I have no difficulty in holding that God may sometimes hear the prayers of sincere pagans, but I fail to see the value of calling them together to pray for world peace. One single sacrifice of the Mass would seem to have more value for that than the prayers of any number of pagans. But I think that it will probably be some time before historians or theologians are able to access his acts and ideas with any hope of understanding them fully.

Ever since the election of Pope Francis in 2013, there has been widespread controversy regarding many of his theological statements such as found in his post-synodal exhortation, Amoris Laetitia, and his encyclical letter of 2015, Laudato Si'. Can we see continuity with his predecessors or is there a striking rupture? It seems that many Catholics are confused by the present pontificate. Can you shed some light on this question?

I have been critical of some of the less clear statements of Pope Francis, for example on marriage, such as are found in some passages in *Amoris Laetitia* and in some of his *ad hoc* replies to questions in interviews, or of his actions and statements regarding the unique truth of the revelation made to mankind in Jesus Christ, and hence the unique place of the Catholic faith — for example, the Abu Dhabi statement or the odd goings on with the statute of Pachamama during the Amazon synod, actions which can only confuse people regardless of what Francis' intentions were. Many of them would seem to be guilty of the sort of vagueness that characterizes what is called by theologians a statement intentionally ambiguous.[1]

But it is absurd to conflate these questionable writings and actions with his criticisms of free-market capitalism or with his encyclical *Laudato Si'*, which is an excellent source of Catholic teaching on the environment. Conservative Catholics, of course, generally did not like any of these, but this is because in general they uphold a kind of classical liberalism and hence support free-market capitalism, industrialism, and so. As to *Laudato Si'*, there is nothing in its teaching which should cause any uneasiness to a Catholic. Indeed, it is an excellent document which applies and faithfully develops Catholic doctrine related to our use and misuse of technology.

I might note that Francis' ambiguous actions and utterances regarding religious truth are unfortunately all too common today. There seems to be a growing reluctance to consider that one religion can actually be true. This, I think,

---

[1] See Ludwig Ott, *Fundamental of Catholic Doctrine* (Rockford, Ill.: TAN Books, 1974), p. 10.

is because religions are widely conceived of as mankind's search for God, but the Catholic faith is founded on God's revelation to mankind. If God had never made a revelation, then certainly religion would have to involve a large amount of guesswork or speculation about the Divine. But if we judge that God has indeed made a revelation, first to the Jews, and then to his Church, that changes the matter entirely.

Akin to this is the strange doctrine or philosophy known as esotericism or sometimes perennialism, which holds that each religion, or at least each traditional major religion, is simply a different path to the unknown Godhead, and each believer ought to follow that religion in which he has been placed. But those in the know, so to speak, realize that whatever religion they practice is only an approximation to divine truth. The parallels of this to Gnosticism are obvious. Lately I've become aware of a certain interest in and attraction to this even in Catholic circles, which is odd indeed. Just as syncretistic beliefs and actions are a temptation for the Catholic Left, it seems that esotericism is a temptation for the Catholic Right. But both are forms of indifferentism and utterly incompatible with adherence to Catholicism. Esotericism, in my opinion, is definitely an elitist position, in the bad sense of that term, likely to appeal to persons with a certain amount of philosophic and historical knowledge — or at least with pretensions to that — but that likely will never become popular. That in fact is probably part of its attraction, that it seems to place one above the run-of-the-mill believer, upon whom the esotericist can look down with a mixture of pity and contempt, or at least, of benign satisfaction that one is above the crude and literal notions that the everyday faithful have.

On a related note, the Second Vatican Council is increasingly being scrutinized by many educated laymen as well as some bishops (e.g., Bishop Athanasius Schneider, Archbishop Carlo Viganò). This criticism is not new of course but given that the debate has not died down, what do you make of this criticism of the Council? Is the problem related to the texts themselves or to its interpretation?

There are a few texts in the Council that raise concerns, especially the decree on religious liberty, *Dignitatis Humanae*. I have argued more than once, especially in my book, *Foundations of a Catholic Political Order*, chap. 2, that this decree can be read in harmony with the teachings of so many popes, up to and including Pius XII, that religious liberty which includes the toleration of religious error, is in itself not something desirable, but that may be permitted or even required in order to avoid a greater evil. I would say the same thing about any other questionable conciliar text: if we can read it in harmony with established doctrine we should do so. Probably there were those among the conciliar Fathers who were hoping to overturn established doctrines, but their private opinions are not controlling for reading the text. Rather, as I noted before, reasonable canons of textual interpretation require that if possible we understand the conciliar documents in an orthodox sense. They are not simply ordinary texts that originate with an author, but, like legal texts, formally reflect a collective mind and must be read as part of a larger body of work, in the case of the Council's documents, as part of the entire magisterial teaching of the Catholic Church. St. Thomas Aquinas, for his part, generally took this approach toward all the authors and texts he made use of, that is, he tried to read apparently conflicting statements in such a way as to eliminate or minimize their differences. Obviously there are limits to such an approach; words and propositions do have meanings. But on the other hand, especially in the kinds of texts we're discussing here, it makes more sense to see if we can reconcile them before we make accusations of conflict.

But if this is so, then what is the origin of the obvious deplorable state of the Church today? Does it have anything to do with Vatican II, or what? Clearly it does, but in complex ways. The Council was obviously a heady experience for participants of all ranks, and there seems to have been a sense that the Holy Spirit was going to remake the Church in important and fundamental ways. So much changed so rapidly immediately after the Council closed — most importantly probably the Roman liturgy itself — that it's no wonder people became confused. It's far from clear to me, though, how and why the unique truth of the Catholic faith and the binding force of the Church's moral teachings suddenly were so widely rejected, and why bishops and others did so little to defend that faith and those moral teachings. Despite their occasional lack of clarity, there's little or nothing in the Conciliar texts themselves that should have caused such a revolution. But whatever the cause, the opening of the Church's windows, as John XXIII expressed it, has certainly allowed errors galore to invade the precincts of the Church, and the way out of this state is far from clear.

As you're aware, the original schemas for the Second Vatican Council were written in a more scholastic or Thomistic sense but were quickly abandoned for a decidedly more pastoral approach. Do you think this was a mistake and could this partly explain why there is ambiguity in many of the Council documents?

Yes, I think that that was definitely a problem. I'm not an expert on the history of the Council, but from what I've read, even before the Council convened there was a difference of opinion and a lack of clarity as to what the Council was supposed to accomplish. The rejection of the original schemas seemed to open the Council to even more uncertainty, and, as you say, to a lack of clarity in the final texts. But this last point should not be overemphasized, for there's little in those texts that could authorize or sanction so much of what has been done "in the spirit of Vatican II."

3
Catholic Social Teaching

Catholic Social Teaching is often written about by those who are often described as "left-leaning" or "right." While those labels do not accurately describe the philosophical thinking behind those positions, why do you think so many groups within the Church have such varying views on it?

Sadly, it is because most Catholics today, at least in the United States, are conservatives or liberals first, and Catholics second. As such, they filter Catholic doctrine, and in particular Catholic social doctrine, through the lens of their political or ideological commitments. As Catholics we are bound to accept and adhere to all that the Church teaches. Some of this teaching has a resonance with what we in the U. S. call the Right, some with the Left, but these are purely accidental resonances. In fact, the Faith and the philosophical and political attitudes which historically it has fostered have different foundations from either conservatism or liberalism, particularly as these terms are used in the United States. In the United States Catholics have long felt inferior to the surrounding Protestant culture and made huge efforts to fit in, to be accepted, to be seen as good Americans. With the almost total collapse of Catholic discipline since the Council, this has allowed most American Catholics to uncritically embrace one or the other of the two cultural-political blocs that predominate in this country, conservatism or liberalism. This has done untold damage to Catholic faith and witness. In fact, I think we can say that a necessary precondition for any effective recovery of Catholic social doctrine in the everyday life and teaching of Catholics is a prior recovery of Catholic identity, of the fact that we should identify first as

Catholics, and any subsequent identity that we might have must not be at odds with our Catholic identity.

But this will be very hard to achieve, since probably the majority of American Catholics are imbued with Americanism, with the idea that the United States is some special and exceptional place, one moreover that just happens to fit well with Catholicism. I'd like to think that among younger Catholics beliefs like this are fading, but I'm not all that sure about this.

This Catholic Americanism has its liberal as well as its conservative variants. The liberal Catholic Americanist likes to think of the U. S. as leading the world in terms of human rights—and now those "human rights" often include the right to abortion, legal recognition of homosexual behavior and relationships, and so on, while the conservative Catholic Americanist thinks of the United States as exporting free markets, technology, and so forth. Both groups, I suppose, like the idea of our exporting electoral democracy, the attainment of which we uncritically view as one of the highpoints of human history, regardless of how well it is working or the quality of those persons whom we elect.

In your book, An Economics of Justice & Charity, *you describe how there is continuity in papal teachings regarding Catholic social teaching. Could you perhaps summarize your argument for readers?*

First a distinction. In its broadest sense, Catholic social teaching concerns the entire social order, political and economic and cultural in the broad sense, and ultimately with the reign of Jesus Christ over the social order. Pius XI, in his first encyclical, *Ubi Arcano,* summarized it as,

> Catholic doctrine on such questions as social authority, the right of owning private property, on the relations between capital and labor, on

the rights of the laboring man, on the relations between Church and State, religion and country, on the relations between the different social classes, on international relations, on the rights of the Holy See and the prerogatives of the Roman Pontiff and the Episcopate, on the social rights of Jesus Christ, Who is the Creator, Redeemer, and Lord not only of individuals but of nations. (no. 60)

Most often, however, people employ the term Catholic social teaching to refer to the Church's teaching on economic morality, and there's nothing especially wrong with that, so long as we remember that that teaching is set in a larger context, and is related to "the social rights of Jesus Christ, Who is the Creator, Redeemer, and Lord not only of individuals but of nations." Using the term in its narrow aspect, then, that is, teaching concerning economic justice, the fundamental question is whether we regard the economy as an essentially self-regulating mechanism or as something that requires intelligent intervention on the part of human beings. Pius XI in *Quadragesimo Anno* put this matter very clearly.

> Just as the unity of human society cannot be founded on an opposition of classes, so also the right ordering of economic life cannot be left to a free competition of forces. For from this source, as from a poisoned spring, have originated and spread all the errors of individualist economic teaching. Destroying through forgetfulness or ignorance the social and moral character of economic life, it held that economic life must be considered and treated as altogether free from and independent of public authority, because in the market, i.e., in the free struggle of competitors, it would have a principle of self direction which

governs it much more perfectly than would the intervention of any created intellect. But free competition, while justified and certainly useful provided it is kept within certain limits, clearly cannot direct economic life—a truth which the outcome of the application in practice of the tenets of this evil individualistic spirit has more than sufficiently demonstrated. (no. 88)

Those who have been influenced by the tradition of economic thought stemming from eighteenth century rationalism want to have in purely market forces "a principle of self direction which governs it much more perfectly than would the intervention of any created intellect." This is a false ideal, and every social encyclical from Leo XIII to Francis has rejected it. Indeed, the patristic and medieval Church earlier rejected this false position as well. Of course not just any intervention by created intellects results in justice or advances the common good. To have effective action that does promote justice and the common good, it is necessary to take account of the many principles of Catholic social teaching contained in the Church's doctrinal patrimony. Moreover, the application of these principles requires experience and intelligence. But the foundation stone upon which they must build is the recognition that intelligent intervention in economic matters to orient the economy toward justice and charity is necessary. It is neither a violation of anyone's economic freedom nor a distortion of so-called market forces.

This has been a constant in Catholic teaching, as I said. In fact, Benedict XVI called attention to the continuity in Catholic social teaching in his own encyclical *Caritas in Veritate*. He wrote,

> The link between *Populorum Progressio* and the Second Vatican Council does not mean that Paul

VI's social magisterium marked a break with that of previous Popes, because the Council constitutes a deeper exploration of this magisterium within the continuity of the Church's life. In this sense, clarity is not served by certain abstract subdivisions of the Church's social doctrine, which apply categories to Papal social teaching that are extraneous to it. It is not a case of two typologies of social doctrine, one pre-conciliar and one post-conciliar, differing from one another: on the contrary, there is a single teaching, consistent and at the same time ever new. It is one thing to draw attention to the particular characteristics of one Encyclical or another, of the teaching of one Pope or another, but quite another to lose sight of the coherence of the overall doctrinal corpus. (no. 12).

It would appear that these remarks were in response to interpretations of John Paul's *Centesimus*, which purported to find in that encyclical a departure from the previous and settled teaching of the Church.

Beyond that there are many specific points made, say by Leo XIII, and especially by Pius XI, that are reiterated by later popes, including by John Paul II. But since the social teachings of the various pontiffs are attempts to give guidance to their contemporaries in the difficulties and perplexities of their own time, it is hardly strange that the specific policies they propose are not identical, for they are dealing with very different times and economic circumstances. For example, the discussion in *Quadragesimo Anno* of Italy's fascist economy, obviously a live issue in 1931, is at most of historical interest today, and equally John Paul's remarks in *Centesimus Annus* on the emerging global capitalism in the wake of the demise of the Soviet bloc.

You've made mention of the 'common good' and it seems to be a crucial principle of Catholic social teaching for the right ordering of society. How would you define it? Who decides what is the common good for society?

John XXIII in his encyclical *Mater et Magistra*, defines the common good as "the sum total of those conditions of social life, by which men are able more fully and more readily to achieve their own perfection."[1] Although it is a *common* good, that doesn't mean it's something alien to individual persons, but rather it's proper to each one of us since it concerns and facilitates our own individual perfection. And since that perfection can normally be achieved only as part of a larger body or, more accurately, as part of various larger bodies, of which the state or *polis* plays the crucial directing role, it's proper to speak of it in terms of "conditions of social life."

As far as the question of who gets to decide what is the common good, this is the sort of question or objection libertarians like to bring up, suggesting that since there is considerable disagreement about what is the good, let alone the common good, any decision imposed by public authority is necessarily arbitrary or tyrannical. But this is a red herring. Laws, for example, always necessitate decisions among different ideas of the good, and someone has to make such laws. In order to establish a libertarian society, for example, some one or some group must decide to do so, and doing so they thereby exclude other ideas of society. In fact, libertarians have their own notion of the common good which they seek to impose on everyone, although they disguise this by arguing that they're simply allowing everyone the maximum freedom to make his own choices. But for those

---

[1] "*quae summam complectitur earum vitae socialis condicionum, quibus homines suam ipsorum perfectionem possint plenius atque expeditius consequi*" (no. 65).

of us who think that society is more than a collection of competing monads, our idea of what is a good society is as effectively excluded by libertarians as they themselves see their understanding of a good society excluded by the choices their opponents would make.

Society needs some ruling authority to make these kinds of decisions. Leo XIII wrote in his encyclical, *Immortale Dei* (no. 3),

> But, as no society can hold together unless some one be over all, directing all to strive earnestly for the common good, every body politic must have a ruling authority, and this authority, no less than society itself, has its source in nature, and has, consequently, God for its Author. Hence, it follows that all public power must proceed from God. For God alone is the true and supreme Lord of the world. Everything, without exception, must be subject to Him, and must serve him, so that whosoever holds the right to govern holds it from one sole and single source, namely, God, the sovereign Ruler of all. "There is no power but from God."

This kind of language grates on the ears of many, especially among English-speakers, but it is part of the patrimony both of Catholic teaching and of sound philosophy. So the quick answer to your question of who decides, is that it is the ruling authority, the government, however that might be constituted, as a democracy or otherwise. Of course, governments, like the rest of us require the guidance of the Church to securely learn what is truly good. The question of how a government receives this knowledge of the good, and so on, is too large a topic to go into here, though.

Is Catholic social teaching more conducive to certain economic models? How do we determine if a certain economic model is compatible with Church teaching? What criteria do we use?

If by "economic model" you mean a basic approach to studying economics and understanding how economies work, such as the neoclassical school, the Austrian school, Institutionalism, the German Historical School, etc., then I think that if you look at the way the popes in their encyclicals have analyzed economic behavior, one would be forced to conclude that by and large they were using as their economic model important elements of the Historical School and of Institutionalism. That is, they did not ignore actual economic history and the outcomes that various historical epochs present in terms of economic justice, and they realized the immense importance of institutions, such as the guilds of the Middle Ages, modern labor unions, etc., in bringing about justice. They constantly speak of the difference that laws and institutions can make in economic outcomes and do not regard the economy as a self-regulating mechanism, as the quote from Pius XI above makes clear. Thus it would seem that the approach of both the neoclassical and the Austrian models, which tend to look upon the economy as a self-regulating mechanism which can be analyzed *a priori*, does not fit well with the kind of economic analysis that is presupposed in the papal social encyclicals.

But if by "economic model" you mean a way of actually organizing an economy, then, yes, certainly, the Church's teaching does mandate certain things, recommend certain things and forbid certain things. As I said, the notion that the economy is a self-regulating mechanism is contrary to what the popes have taught. So some kind of intervention is necessary to orient the economy toward justice and charity. However, this intervention need not be done by the central government, and in fact should be done by lower bodies where that is feasible. Most often the approach that Catholic social doctrine takes is at odds with both contemporary conservatives (or neo-liberals) and liberals (or social democrats), both of which ideologies assume that the greater or lesser role of the central state is the point at issue.

The Austrian School finds many Catholic adherents. Why do you think it attracts so many Catholics and why is it problematic?

Many students of economics see some of the problems with the regnant neoclassical school and turn to the most readily available alternative, which is the Austrian school. At least, I would suppose that was a major reason for its popularity. Also, it validates people's preexisting predilection for a minimal state, for an essentially free-market or *laissez-faire* economy, and appears to give a scientific justification for that predilection. But in fact, Austrian economics suffers from the same chief defects as does neoclassical economics, a deductive approach that ignores actual economic facts and economic history. Also, it is based upon a severely defective philosophical foundation, as even some of its Catholic proponents admit.[2] Ludwig von Mises, one of the main proponents of the Austrian school, "associated himself, especially in *Human Action* (1949), with Epicureanism and utilitarianism," as Gregg notes. But Mises does more than that, for example his dismissal of religion as "pompous statements which people make about things unknowable and beyond the power of the human mind, their cosmologies, world views, religions, mysticisms, metaphysics, and conceptual phantasies...."[3]

Libertarianism, as a political philosophy, seems to appeal to

---

2 See Samuel Gregg, "Markets, Catholicism, and Libertarianism," *Public Discourse*, October 25, 2016, at https://www.thepublicdiscourse.com/2016/10/18112/
3 *Human Action*, pp. 180–81.

many Catholics who don't think in such a dichotomous fashion as "Democrat" or "Republican." Are there any problems with this political philosophy?

Libertarianism is the philosophy underlying the Austrian school, which I just mentioned. It is the same as the liberal ideology that Pius XI (and many other popes) spoke of, and as such it simply stands condemned by the Church's teaching authority. Pius wrote,

> With regard to civil authority, Leo XIII, boldly breaking through the confines imposed by Liberalism, fearlessly taught that government must not be thought a mere guardian of law and of good order, but rather must put forth every effort so that "through the entire scheme of laws and institutions... both public and individual well-being may develop spontaneously out of the very structure and administration of the State." Just freedom of action must, of course, be left both to individual citizens and to families, yet only on condition that the common good be preserved and wrong to any individual be abolished. The function of the rulers of the State, moreover, is to watch over the community and its parts; but in protecting private individuals in their rights, chief consideration ought to be given to the weak and the poor. "For the nation, as it were, of the rich is guarded by its own defenses and is in less need of governmental protection, whereas the suffering multitude, without the means to protect itself relies especially on the protection of the State. Wherefore, since wageworkers are numbered among the great mass of the needy, the State must include them under its special care and foresight." (*Quadragesimo Anno*, no. 5)

Similarly Paul VI wrote in his apostolic letter *Octogesima Adveniens,*

> Therefore the Christian who wishes to live his faith in a political activity which he thinks of as service cannot without contradicting himself adhere to ideological systems which radically or substantially go against his faith and his concept of man. He cannot adhere to the Marxist ideology, to its atheistic materialism, to its dialectic of violence and to the way it absorbs individual freedom in the collectivity, at the same time denying all transcendence to man and his personal and collective history; nor can be adhere to the liberal ideology which believes it exalts individual freedom by withdrawing it from every limitation, by stimulating it through exclusive seeking of interest and power, and by considering social solidarities as more or less automatic consequences of individual initiatives, not as an aim and a major criterion of the value of the social organization. (no. 26)

And later in the same document he writes "that at the very root of philosophical liberalism is an erroneous affirmation of the autonomy of the individual in his activity, his motivation and the exercise of his liberty" (no. 35). In fact, this approach to social theory is radically at variance with historic Catholic socio-political ideas and practices, including how these matters were organized in the Middle Ages, when a serious attempt was made to establish a society which embodied and reflected Catholic ideals in all areas of life. The libertarian ideal of society is, in fact, radically at odds with any Catholic conception of society, in both the political and economic spheres. Catholics who are attracted to it are often ignorant of how different was the spirit of medieval politics and economics, how a notion of the exaltation of individual freedom was utterly foreign to their life and thought. The fact that there is any sizeable number of Catholics for whom libertarianism (or the liberal ideology) is a temptation, shows the gigantic difference between modernity and any traditional Catholic society, and how most of us today are imprisoned in modern thought without being aware of it.

Does the Church teach that there is a particular way an economy should be ordered? If so, why should the world heed the Church?

Yes, but in saying this, we need to look at the entire corpus of Catholic social doctrine. More than once the popes have spoken of the place of Catholic social teaching and its relationship to economics and economic models. Pius XI in *Quadragesimo Anno* said the following,

> 41. Yet before proceeding to explain these matters, that principle which Leo XIII so clearly established must be laid down at the outset here, namely, that there resides in Us the right and duty to pronounce with supreme authority upon social and economic matters. Certainly the Church was not given the commission to guide men to an only fleeting and perishable happiness but to that which is eternal. Indeed" the Church holds that it is unlawful for her to mix without cause in these temporal concerns"; however, she can in no wise renounce the duty God entrusted to her to interpose her authority, not of course in matters of technique for which she is neither suitably equipped nor endowed by office, but in all things that are connected with the moral law. For as to these, the deposit of truth that God committed to Us and the grave duty of disseminating

and interpreting the whole moral law, and of urging it in season and out of season, bring under and subject to Our supreme jurisdiction not only social order but economic activities themselves.

John Paul II in *Laborem Exercens*, no. 41, explained this further,

> The Church's social doctrine is not a "third way" between liberal capitalism and Marxist collectivism, nor even a possible alternative to other solutions less radically opposed to one another: rather, it constitutes a category of its own. Nor is it an ideology, but rather the accurate formulation of the results of a careful reflection on the complex realities of human existence, in society and in the international order, in the light of faith and of the Church's tradition. Its main aim is to interpret these realities, determining their conformity with or divergence from the lines of the Gospel teaching on man and his vocation, a vocation which is at once earthly and transcendent; its aim is thus to guide Christian behavior. It therefore belongs to the field, not of ideology, but of theology and particularly of moral theology.

And finally in *Centesimus Annus*, John Paul wrote,

> 43. The Church has no models to present; models that are real and truly effective can only arise within the framework of different historical situations, through the efforts of all those who responsibly confront concrete problems in all their social, economic, political and cultural aspects, as these interact with one another.

Now these statements are liable to misinterpretation, and the entire body of papal social doctrine must be taken into account when we try to understand them. Essentially they are saying that the ethical mandates which the Church takes, mostly from the natural law, apply "not only to the social order but to economic activities themselves." Thus the economy is not some sphere of human activity independent of morality. But the Church does not offer technical solutions, for example, a complete model of how to construct a just economy. In fact, as John Paul says, "models that are real and truly effective can only arise within the framework of different historical situations." Concrete situations differ so much in place and time that the details of how to organize economic activity are bound to be different in different places and times. But the Church does offer an "accurate formulation of the results of a careful reflection on the complex realities of human existence, in society and in the international order, in the light of faith and of the Church's tradition." Thus the fundamental principles of a just economic order will be the same always and everywhere.

But as I've said more than once already, we need to actually look at the corpus of the social encyclicals, in which we will find numerous concrete proposals, suggestions and prohibitions, some of them having more authority than others, to be sure.

You ask, "why should the world heed the Church?" That, of course, would depend upon the world examining, understanding and being convinced of the value of the Church's social thought. Right now this is not being done very much, though there is some interest by non-Catholics in distributism. Sadly, though, too many Catholics do not even heed the Church on these matters. The Church needs to recover her confidence and her voice and not be hesitant to proclaim her social teaching—as indeed, all of her teaching.

Distributism seems to produce a variety of reactions among its critics from the idea that it is nothing but romanticism and mere "dress-up" into a fantasy world to the idea that it is too wedded in a socialist philosophy because it, they would argue, is too centralized in its approach and seeks to force the wider distribution of wealth. You have written extensively on this question but could you perhaps give the readers a synopsis of distributism, its origins and how it represents an authentically Catholic understanding of social and economic issues?

Distributism is an economic system, and to a lesser extent an entire social system, that for the sake of stability and justice seeks to decentralize the economy as much as is practical. In particular distributism favor widespread property ownership, either by individuals or families, or in some form of worker ownership when technology or the necessity for large amounts of capital make individual ownership impractical. It originated in the early 20th century with writers such as Hilaire Belloc and G. K. Chesterton, but was similar to other economic movements of that time. Chesterton's younger brother, Cecil gave what is probably the best definition of distributism when he wrote,

> A Distributist is a man who desires that the means of production should, generally speaking, remain private property, but that their ownership should be so distributed that the determining mass of families—ideally every family—should have an efficient share therein. That is Distributism, and nothing else is Distributism.... Distributism is quite as possible in an industrial or commercial as in an agrarian community.... [4]

---

[4] Cecil Chesterton, "Shaw and My Neighbour's Chimney," *The New Witness*, May 3, 1917, p. 13. Quoted in Race Mathews, *Jobs of Our Own: Building a Stakeholder Society*, (Distributist Review Press: Irving, Texas, 2d ed., 2009), p. 101.

If we take a close look at distributism and capitalism, we will be able to see the superiority of the former and why there are legitimate objections to the latter. A few years ago I wrote the following:

> Capitalism, which Pope Pius XI characterized in *Quadragesimo Anno*, no. 100, as the separation of ownership and work, as "that economic system in which were provided by different people the capital and labor jointly needed for production," has at its heart a contradiction or built-in conflict. While the separation of ownership and work is not necessarily unjust, when it becomes the dominant method of economic organisation in a society it becomes dangerous in that a sharp divide is created around the labor market. For some, the owners, who are now at least partly divorced from the actual process of production, economic activity tends to become simply a means of personal enrichment via the production of whatever will sell, regardless of whether it helps or hurts the common good. And for these owners, labor is now chiefly an item of expense; hence the pressure to reduce labor costs as much as possible. But what for capitalists are labor costs, for workers is a living, their living and that of their families. Moving a factory to a cheaper location may seem to make sense for someone who merely supplies the capital necessary for production, but it can hardly make sense for someone who depends on that factory for the job that supports himself and his family. When ownership of the means of production is distributed among workers and families, then other factors besides the purely economic enter into every economic decision. In an economic downturn, for

example, workers who are at the same time owners will naturally look upon themselves and their families as more than mere "labor costs," and hence consider other options besides simply layoffs or plant closings. They will see the economic factors as part of a complex of factors which necessarily impact much more than questions of money. Each person's family, immediate and extended, his friendships, his parish, his attachment to his own locale, and so on, are quite as relevant considerations as the level of profit that can be made in any particular place. Indeed, unless those who make such decisions consider more than merely economic factors, they can hardly be regarded as human beings. They are mere calculating machines, and their work can be just as efficiently performed by some sort of electronic device. But as long as the capitalist economic structure is in place, the mass of workers will not even have the opportunity to consider such non-economic factors or make these kinds of decisions.[5]

Distributism, then, seeks to orient economic activity towards its proper and inherent end, not speculation, not enrichment for its own sake, not the unlimited use of natural resources, but the supply of our needs and reasonable desires. The economy ought to be a subordinate factor in social life, important, yes, but always subordinate to the overall needs and purposes of society, whose ultimate purpose is assisting us on our journey toward eternal life with God. Yes, we need to use and consume goods and services, yes, the desire for a sufficient amount of worldly goods is legitimate

---

5 Distributism? — or, Three Acres and a Cow? *The Chesterton Review*, vol. 44, nos. 1-2, spring/summer 2018, pp. 77–87.

and reasonable, but the desire for as much as possible, for simply fulfilling every human whim is not reasonable, nor is it healthy either for society or for the natural environment.

One of the biggest objections that the critics of distributism have concerns how we would establish a distributist economy. In his book, *The Restoration of Property*, Belloc recommended a rate of taxation of concentrated property that would, in effect, compel owners of large amounts of productive property to sell off their excess in order to bring about a more desirable distributism of property. I do not think this is wrong, nor, as far as I know, has the Church ever condemned it. But it may be impractical, at least in a country such as the United States. Other methods have been suggested. For example, in his recent book, *Distributism Basics*, David Cooney wrote,

> It is also important to remember that other ideas are possible. To accomplish the wider distribution of large properties already held, we could use the opportunity of future transfers of ownership. If dealing with a large amount of land, there could be a requirement to sell it as several parcels to members of the community. If dealing instead with a large company that has a dominance in a single market or is a necessarily large operation like some forms of manufacturing, a requirement could be made that the new ownership be a cooperative. Again, these are sales voluntarily made by the existing owners; they are not forced to sell what they already own. If dealing with a large company operating in multiple markets, say books and clothing, each could be required to be sold as a separate business so that, where there was one company with one owner (or set of owners), there

are now multiple businesses with different owners. This allows the current owner to keep a business already legally owned and to pass it on to his heirs. This allows that owner to sell it for profit or need. This also accomplishes the wider distribution of property when the owner chooses to sell.[6]

If we recognize that the economy has a purpose, and that like all purposes this places limitations on the activity in question, we will see that distributism does not restrict any legitimate economic freedom. It does insist, however, that the economy be subordinated to the common good of society. Everyone should have the freedom to engage in economic activity according to the purpose of that activity, namely, to allow us to provide for the external goods and services we need to live. But no one has the right to engage in economic activity that is harmful to the common good. This is a disordered freedom, and the public authorities, or occupational associations such as guilds, have every right to restrict or prohibit it. As Pius XI wrote in *Quadragesimo Anno* with regard to the disordered economic activity of early capitalism:

> 133. Strict and watchful moral restraint enforced vigorously by governmental authority could have banished these enormous evils and even forestalled them; this restraint, however, has too often been sadly lacking. For since the seeds of a new form of economy were bursting forth just when the principles of rationalism had been implanted and rooted in many minds, there quickly developed a body of economic teaching far removed from the true moral law, and, as a result, completely free rein was given to human passions.

---

6   Page 55. (Available from TheBookPatch.com)

> 134. Thus it came to pass that many, much more than ever before, were solely concerned with increasing their wealth by any means whatsoever, and that in seeking their own selfish interests before everything else they had no conscience about committing even the gravest of crimes against others. Those first entering upon this broad way that leads to destruction easily found numerous imitators of their iniquity by the example of their manifest success, by their insolent display of wealth, by their ridiculing the conscience of others, who, as they said, were troubled by silly scruples, or lastly by crushing more conscientious competitors.

Although I have long been a promoter of distributism, we should not forget that there are other authentic Catholic attempts at establishing a just economic framework for the modern world, in particular the system of solidarism associated with Fr. Heinrich Pesch (1854–1926), a towering figure in Catholic social thought. Solidarism, in my opinion, differs from distributism mostly in emphasis, and there is considerable overlap between how each of them would try to organize an economy and a just social order.

Could you describe how the trajectory towards a "capitalistic" economy came about in much of the Western world? Was there a 'moment' when Western society could have chosen otherwise?

The rise of capitalism was a long and complex process. But it was hardly inevitable. Pius XI spoke to this point in *Quadragesimo Anno*:

> For there was a social order once which, although indeed not perfect or in all respects ideal, nevertheless, met in a certain measure the requirements of

right reason, considering the conditions and needs of the time. If that order has long since perished, that surely did not happen because the order could not have accommodated itself to changed conditions and needs by development and by a certain expansion, but rather because men, hardened by too much love of self, refused to open the order to the increasing masses as they should have done, or because, deceived by allurements of a false freedom and other errors, they became impatient of every authority and sought to reject every form of control. (no. 97)

In fact, it was governmental and legal action that enabled and permitted the capitalist system to arise and become established. Critics of distributism like to pretend that a capitalist economy is somehow the natural economy for mankind, but this is entirely false. If we look, for example, at the rise of corporations, that is, limited liability companies, particularly in the United States, we see that they are purely creations of the legal system, and the rights that they claim, corporate personhood, for example, were granted by a complicit legal system, and could not exist were it not for that continuing sanction. Or if we consider the concept of the free market, it usually is understood as a market in which anything except force or fraud, both narrowly interpreted, is permitted. But this is arbitrary. Why is not an image of a genuine free market a crowd of shoppers fighting over the last few new electronic gadgets on sale at some big box store? If it is replied that force and fraud are wrong, so are all actions that harm the common good. In the Middle Ages many anti-social acts were prohibited, such as attempting to corner the market in raw materials, selling substandard products, and so on. These are as much against the natural law or the natural purpose of an economy as outright force or fraud. Any economic system requires a legal framework to support it, and capitalism is no exception. Many things that are considered commonplace today would have been prohibited by medieval laws or guild regulations, and to work to restore these laws and regulations is an entirely reasonable and just activity, and one especially appropriate for the Catholic laity as part of our duty to reform the social order in the light of the Gospel.

What in fact were some of the economic practices prohibited or regulated in the medieval period? I am not thinking of the obvious examples of certain individual moral behavior but more in terms of economic activity or political life.

I'll give some examples of specific practices, but it's important to recognize and remember that economic life was carried on in a completely different spirit from today. Economic activity was embedded in social life as a whole, it existed to further the good of society by supplying necessary or useful external goods, not as a means of enriching the most clever or the most conniving or even the most hard-working economic actor. I mentioned a few of these specific prohibited practices just now, among them the prohibition of *forestalling*, the practice of buying up all the raw material necessary for a particular trade — say, by meeting a ship when it was unloading a particular product and buying up the whole lot of something needed for manufacturing a finished product before other craftsmen could get their share. Then, of course, the prohibition of *usury*. And usury means not simply lending money at a high rate of interest, but lending money at *any* rate of interest, simply on the basis that it was a loan. There were certainly ways in which interest could justly be charged, for example, to cover losses or make good opportunities a lender might miss while his money was out on loan, and as time went on various contrivances were invented to facilitate loans at interest and evade the severe canonical penalties for usury, for example, the triple contract (*contractus trinus*), but still the doctrine that usury was immoral helped give a different tone and direction to economic life.

Then there were the *guilds*, probably the most important of the medieval institutions which impacted economic life, to which craftsmen working in a particular city were usually required to belong. They regulated prices, product quality, prohibited working at certain times, sometimes put limits on the number of apprentices a master craftsman could have, and endeavored to foster a spirit of cooperation among those working in the same trade. One historian summed up the role of guilds in this way:

> A guild was a federation of autonomous workshops, whose owners (the masters) normally made all decisions and established the requirements for promotion from the lower ranks (journeymen or hired helpers, and apprentices). Inner conflicts were usually minimized by a common interest in the welfare of the craft and a virtual certitude that sooner or later every proficient apprentice and industrious journeyman would become a master and share in the governance of the craft. To make sure that expectations would be fulfilled, a guild would normally forbid overtime work after dark and sometimes limit the number of dependents a master could employ; this also served to maintain substantial equality among masters and to prevent overexpansion of the craft.[7]

---

7 Robert S. Lopez, *The Commercial Revolution of the Middle Ages, 950–1350*. (Cambridge: Cambridge University, 1976), p. 127.

Though greed certainly existed in the Middle Ages it was not officially sanctioned, greed was not advertised as the motive and mainspring of economic life as it now so often is. Economic life and economic motives were firmly embedded within the larger motives which comprise all of social life, and ultimately relate to our desire to achieve eternal life with God.

Criticism of "capitalism" is seen as a characteristic of socialism or communism—if accurate—but would it be appropriate to argue that according to a Catholic conception of life 'capitalism' presents many obstacles? Perhaps it would also benefit readers to define what capitalism is since it seems to be a term rife with confusion.

The controlling text for answering your question is found in *Quadragesimo Anno*.

> 100. You know, Venerable Brethren and Beloved Children, that the Encyclical of Our Predecessor of happy memory [Leo XIII's *Rerum Novarum*] had in view chiefly that economic system, wherein, generally, some provide capital while others provide labor for a joint economic activity. And in a happy phrase he described it thus: "Neither capital can do without labor, nor labor without capital."

> 101. With all his energy Leo XIII sought to adjust this economic system according to the norms of right order; hence, it is evident that this system is not to be condemned in itself. And surely it is not of its own nature vicious. But it does violate right order when capital hires workers, that is, the non-owning working class, with a view to and

under such terms that it directs business and even the whole economic system according to its own will and advantage, scorning the human dignity of the workers, the social character of economic activity and social justice itself, and the common good.

Here we find the most adequate definition of capitalism, as "that economic system, wherein, generally, some provide capital while others provide labor for a joint economic activity," and at the same time the judgment that "this system is not to be condemned in itself." This is important. It is not unjust for someone to hire others to work for him, provided of course that he pays a just wage and observes the other stipulations of social doctrine.

But on the other hand, a Catholic is free to think that capitalism, precisely because of this separation of ownership and work, is unwise and historically has inflicted huge amounts of damage on the social fabric. Part of the reason for this is put in a quote from Hilaire Belloc that I have used more than once in my writing.

> But wealth obtained indirectly as profit out of other men's work, or by process of exchange, becomes a thing abstracted from the process of production. As the interest of a man in things diminishes, his interest in abstract wealth—money—increases. The man who makes a table or grows a crop makes the success of the crop or the table a test of excellence.
>
> The intermediary who buys and sells the crop or the table is not concerned with the goodness of table or crop, but with the profit he makes between their purchase and sale. In a productive society the superiority of the things produced is the measure of success: in a Commercial society

the amount of wealth accumulated by the dealer is the measure of success.[8]

If the purpose of economic activity is to supply humanity with the goods and services we need for a decent human life, then economic activity ought to be focused on that primary task, not on schemes for more and more moneymaking. Those who are removed one or more steps from the productive process generally will look on economic activity as simply a means for profit, rather than on a reasonable profit as a byproduct of one's work. Thus Catholic distributists believe that capitalism is an unwise system, but they do not, or ought not, to hold that capitalism as it is here defined is intrinsically evil, since Pius XI makes clear here that this is not so.

It's important to note, moreover, that capitalism, while essentially consisting in the separation of ownership and work, can and does exist in many different forms. The German social market economy, for example, which seems to be the object of John Paul II's encomium in *Centesimus Annus*, no. 19, as "a positive effort to rebuild a democratic society inspired by social justice," with its elaborate system of co-determination does much to make capitalism operate in a just manner that does not violate the common good. The same cannot be said for capitalism as it operates in the United States, though, which John Paul in the same passage criticizes as "the affluent society or the consumer society [which] seeks to defeat Marxism on the level of pure materialism by showing how a free-market society can achieve a greater satisfaction of material human needs than Communism, while equally excluding spiritual values [and which] agrees with Marxism, in the sense that it totally reduces man to the sphere of economics and the satisfaction of material needs."

---

8   *An Essay on the Nature of Contemporary England* (New York: Sheed & Ward, 1937), p. 67.

Also we should note, that *free-market* capitalism, an economy in which "free competition" is the ruling principle, is specifically condemned as wrong by the Church. See *Quadragesimo Anno*, no. 88, which I quoted before.

Can you give some concrete examples of the way capitalism works in the United States that makes it more problematic?

Though there are obviously some prohibitions against totally unfettered competition in this country, they are much fewer and of less importance than are found in many other countries. The contrast with German co-determination is most striking, for in that system there are complex mechanisms to promote cooperation between management and labor and even among different firms by mandating industry-wide union contracts, for example. In the U. S. employment is generally "at will," that is, an employee can be fired for any or no reason, except for certain specific non-discrimination protections written into law in recent decades. Unions here have little power, and are regarded by most employers as a nuisance, rather than as a legitimate economic partner which aids in establishing not only justice, but industrial peace and, as a result, promoting efficiency in production. Slightly over half the states have "right-to-work" laws, which prohibit union shops, that is, they hamper the ability of unions to negotiate with employers on behalf of the entire workforce.

The U. S. minimum wage is a joke, in no way does it approach a true living wage, and in the absence of effective union action or widespread worker ownership a legally mandated minimum wage is a necessity. Even paid vacations are not mandated here, nor employer-provided health insurance (since there is no governmental system for that). But I emphasize that it's the spirit of American capitalism that's not only responsible for the legal framework that we have, but for the way in which employers too often regard their employees, that is, simply as cost items in their accounting, not as human beings with their own legitimate needs and aspirations.

What do you think are the biggest challenges for the concrete application of Catholic social teaching in society? Is it even possible anymore?

First, of course, Catholics themselves have to be convinced that Catholic social doctrine is true and that is it something which could reasonably be implemented, not some pie-in-the-sky plan that's nice on paper but has no applicability in the real world. As I've already noted here, Catholics by and large are both ignorant of the Church's doctrine on the social order, and in fact tend to reject it or large parts of it.

Then, another very major challenge is our lack of willingness to seriously consider a radical change to our socio-economic system. Certainly it's possible—if we were willing to make the effort, both the intellectual effort to think matters through, and the practical effort to undertake its application. If we had the will to do so, the many practical problems of how to apply Catholic doctrine to a reform of the economy or social order could certainly be overcome.

In addition, Catholics are of course a minority in this country, and serious Catholics are a minority in every country. So first of all one would have to convince enough Catholics or people of good will to listen to the Church's voice. And of course entrenched interests would make the effort to apply Catholic social teaching very difficult indeed. The power of corporations, for example, is immense, and they fight bitterly against any attempt to weaken their power and lessen their income.

Catholic Social Teaching

While it is true that Catholics constitute a minority both in the United States and the world, and an even smaller number actively practice their faith, still would you say that it is a failure of Catholics to integrate their faith into daily life that has produced, or at least contributed to, the neglect of Catholic social doctrine, and to the failure to put it into practice? If even a million Catholics rejected the spirit of the world, then maybe Catholic social teaching could become a principle with great force in society.

Let us speak first of the United States. Right now Catholics in this country are bitterly divided, but divided in pretty much the same manner as the rest of the country is. Our religious beliefs do not seem to mean much when we so eagerly join with one or the other of the two political-cultural blocs, that is, liberals or conservatives, that dominate American life and thought. So right now, as you certainly recognize, any attempt to put social teaching into practice would mostly result in two competing versions, even two competing errors. This is not to say, however, that there are not some people who do have a genuine Catholic vision, but they are few and far between, and not able to do much.

But there is another point that is very important. Catholic social teaching is teaching about society, and while there is much that individuals or small groups can do, any reading of the social encyclicals makes it clear that there is much that has to be done on the level of society as a whole, and hence, in one way or another, must involve the political. So, yes, if "a million Catholics rejected the spirit of the world" that would surely have consequences that we could not foresee, still at some point there would have to be action at the political level. The rise of labor unions is perhaps a good example. The Church had always more or less supported them, and they are a very crucial part of the application of Catholic social teaching—at least in a capitalist economy. But it took political action at the national level—the Wagner Act of 1935, to make union organizing effective and widespread.

Another example. One of the key points of Hilaire Belloc's program to establish distributism was a tax on chain stores, as I already mentioned. Not many people know that in the United States, after World War I, numerous states actually enacted such laws on behalf of small and independent businesses, albeit these taxes were not as steeply graduated as Belloc advocated.

The U.S. Congress even held hearings on proposed national legislation to regulate chain stores in the early 1940s. Obviously this movement did not ultimately triumph, but my point here is that political action was necessary to establish this key point in Catholic social teaching. Similarly, if we ever attempted to establish occupational groups or guilds we would need more than "a million Catholics who reject the spirit of the world." We would need organization, and we would even need political action, for example, major changes in anti-trust laws.

In his 1937 encyclical, *Divini Redemptoris,* Pius XI speaks of the necessity for joint action in order to realize something like a just social order, and of the frequent helplessness of individuals to achieve this.

> It happens all too frequently, however, under the salary system, that individual employers are helpless to ensure justice unless, with a view to its practice, they organize institutions the object of which is to prevent competition incompatible with fair treatment for the workers. Where this is true, it is the duty of contractors and employers to support and promote such necessary organizations as normal instruments enabling them to fulfill their obligations of justice.... (no. 53)

If, therefore, We consider the whole structure of economic life, as We have already pointed out in Our Encyclical *Quadragesimo Anno*, the reign of mutual collaboration between justice and charity in social-economic relations can only be achieved by a body of professional and inter professional organizations, built on solidly Christian foundations.... (no. 54)

The fact that effective work on behalf of social justice requires joint action, even action at the political level, and the obvious difficulty of persuading others to participate in this, is an indication that we would need more than "a million Catholics [who] rejected the spirit of the world," we would need coordinated action that eventually would require important legal and cultural changes in order to establish "a body of professional and inter professional organizations, built on solidly Christian foundations." On the other hand, if we did have those "million Catholics" who were committed to the realization of Catholic social principles, that would obviously be an excellent starting point, but only if those Catholics were able to work together, including supporting the necessary political action.

Why do you think the Church's social teaching has been so buried—in general—among many of its members?

Historically, in part because as I just suggested, its implementation necessarily involved coordinated action, including on the part of the public authorities, and most people probably did not feel that they could contribute much in that respect. And of course, simply spiritual and moral laziness. Moreover, since the United States is a Protestant country, obviously the majority of the population was not disposed to adhere to something taught by a Church they did not themselves adhere to—and regarded not only as erroneous, but (especially in the past) gravely heretical and as a betrayal of Christianity as they knew it.

Today it's even worse, of course, as Catholics generally identify with one of the major political-cultural blocs in this country, and neither of these blocs is interested in implementing Catholic social teaching or reforming society after the precepts of the Gospel, as Pius XI called for in *Quadragesimo Anno*. But we shouldn't forget the real efforts to implement this teaching on the part of Catholics in the past. Aside from purely intellectual or theoretical activity—books, articles, and so on—we should not forget the activity of Catholics involved in public affairs, such as Philip Murray, long-time union leader and president of the CIO, who worked to implement some of the proposals in Pius XI's *Quadragesimo Anno*. Unfortunately Murray's efforts did not achieve much, but in the era of the 1930s and 40s there were numerous Catholics, including clergy, who were involved in union organizing and who supported striking workers. It was indeed a golden age for Catholic social teaching in action.

What do you think of the work of Dorothy Day and Peter Maurin who founded the Catholic Worker in that "golden age for Catholic social teaching in action"? Where do they stand in American Catholic history?

I have great admiration for both of these figures, and I consider Dorothy Day to have been a saint—certainly her holiness shines through her words and actions. At the same time, I cannot agree with certain positions of the Catholic Worker movement, primarily its pacifism and the anarchism she sometimes claimed to espouse. But in both cases I don't know that her thinking was all that clear. I don't think she really was an anarchist, and I don't know whether she rejected merely modern warfare—certainly a defensible position for a Catholic to take—or warfare altogether, which doesn't seem like a position compatible with orthodoxy. She was against World War II, for example, but would she have counseled the Poles just to sit back and allow the Germans to invade and ravage their country in 1939? A war, especially a war extensive in time and place, such as World War II, can be just in certain respects, unjust in others. The extensive bombing of cities carried out by both sides, and especially the atomic bombs, clearly cannot be justified, but I don't think it was wrong for countries to resist the Nazi invasions.

And while obviously the Catholic Worker movement has done a huge amount of good in regard to the corporal works of mercy, as I mentioned before, any real change in the social order has got to involve the state and therefore to involve political action.

An important principle to me seems to be the concept of subsidiarity. Can you briefly define what it is and how it might be an important idea for Catholics and especially for those in positions of authority?

It is worthwhile to quote the entire passage from Pius XI's *Quadragesimo Anno* in order to understand what the principle of subsidiarity really is. Pius wrote,

> 79. As history abundantly proves, it is true that on account of changed conditions many things which were done by small associations in former times cannot be done now save by large associations. *Still, that most weighty principle, which cannot be set aside or changed, remains fixed and unshaken in social philosophy: Just as it is gravely wrong to take from individuals what they can accomplish by their own initiative and*

industry and give it to the community, so also it is an injustice and at the same time a grave evil and disturbance of right order to assign to a greater and higher association what lesser and subordinate organizations can do. For every social activity ought of its very nature to furnish help to the members of the body social, and never destroy and absorb them. [my emphasis]

80. The supreme authority of the State ought, therefore, to let subordinate groups handle matters and concerns of lesser importance, which would otherwise dissipate its efforts greatly. Thereby the State will more freely, powerfully, and effectively do all those things that belong to it alone because it alone can do them: directing, watching, urging, restraining, as occasion requires and necessity demands. Therefore, those in power should be sure that the more perfectly a graduated order is kept among the various associations, in observance of the principle of "subsidiary function," the stronger social authority and effectiveness will be the happier and more prosperous the condition of the State.

81. First and foremost, the State and every good citizen ought to look to and strive toward this end: that the conflict between the hostile classes be abolished and harmonious cooperation of the Industries and Professions be encouraged and promoted [*concors « ordinum » conspiratio excitetur et provehatur*].

82. The social policy of the State, therefore, must devote itself to the re-establishment of the Industries and Professions. In actual fact, human society

now, for the reason that it is founded on classes with divergent aims and hence opposed to one another and therefore inclined to enmity and strife, continues to be in a violent condition and is unstable and uncertain.

The part that I put in italics is often quoted out of context, and is either narrowly applied to governmental functions, e.g., in the United States to the various levels of government, federal, state, local, or even applied by way of contrasting governmental activity with merely private associations or even private businesses. But as can be seen from the context, Pope Pius is primarily talking about a revival of guilds, "Industries and Professions," as he makes clearer in his encyclical, *Divini Redemptoris*, nos. 32, 53, 54. That is, most economic regulation would be done by these guilds, private associations in the sense that they are not to be departments of the government at any level, but not purely voluntary associations either. Rather, as with the medieval guilds, all who engaged in a particular kind of economic activity would automatically be part of a particular guild, and would be bound by the guild's decisions. These would be enforced, if need be, by state authority. In the United States, the closest thing we've come to having such guilds were the Code Authorities established by the National Recovery Administration, an early New Deal effort that was unfortunately struck down by the U. S. Supreme Court.

So adherence to the principle of subsidiarity, in its primary meaning, has nothing to do with the scope or activities of for-profit entities, but rather the guilds or occupational groups or industry councils (as they were sometimes called in this country), organizations that do not exist today, at least in the United States, except as marginal players in society, such as bar associations.

4

Liberalism

You kindly translated Louis Cardinal Billot's work on Liberalism for Arouca Press as well as offering an excellent introduction to situate this work for the American context. Could you briefly describe what "liberalism" is and why it poses such a problem for the individual and society?

I defined, or better, characterized, liberalism in an article in this way.

> Liberalism is that general movement in Western civilization, which has sought freedom from the restraints imposed by Christian teaching, and therefore has attacked Catholic culture, first on the level of Christian economic morality, secondly on the level of the political rights of God, and lastly on the level of the human person itself.[1]

A perceptive reader will notice that liberalism understood in this way is not the same as that term is used in current American political discourse. Yes, American liberalism is certainly a part of this more general liberalism, but it's only one part. American conservatism is likewise a part of that liberalism. Almost everyone who labels himself a conservative in the U. S. is really a liberal. Sometimes we see individuals who are full-blown liberals, in that they embrace the errors of both American liberals and American conservatives. I'm thinking of people like Milton Friedman or Ludwig von Mises.

Above I quoted Paul VI that "that at the very root of philosophical liberalism is an erroneous affirmation of the

---

[1] "Liberalism's Three Assaults," *Homiletic & Pastoral Review*, January 2000.

autonomy of the individual in his activity, his motivation and the exercise of his liberty." Liberalism teaches, explicitly or implicitly, individual freedom in all areas of life, social or personal. Thus it undermines religious authority and, ultimately, even the norms of natural morality, as I mentioned before. It is an enemy of the Catholic conception of life and community, just as much as a totalitarian conception is.

Liberalism, moreover is animated by a great and powerful myth. I said above that it seeks "freedom from the restraints imposed by Christian teaching." In fact, central to it is the myth of the progressive liberalization of mankind from any and all restraints which do not originate within or from the individual himself. In this sense it is against all order, all *form* in a way, not just against the political or economic restraints that medieval civilization imposed upon Europe. Above I spoke of how the efforts toward sexual liberation in the 1960s almost immediately became disordered, embracing even same-sex relationships, and now, more perversely, transgenderism. That is because liberalism is not seeking some ideal state, some ideal of a just order. No, it is always progressing, but progressing toward what? No one knows, not even its own proponents, for they are always discovering new horizons, new restraints which must be broken down and from which we must be freed. And strangely enough, it can even reject what it embraced yesterday and *vice versa*. For example, in the early nineteenth century liberals embraced economic freedom, i.e., free competition as the way to organize an economy. This was a throwing-off of a previous "shackle" which had been imposed by the medieval guilds or the mercantilist policies of governments, but today, and for some time, liberals as a whole have rejected such a *laissez-faire* economic policy. But have they changed their minds and do they now accept the medieval economic order, or something like it, as an ideal? No, certainly not.

Many of them, of course, are unaware of how the Middle Ages organized economic matters, but even when they are cognizant of it, they reject it because it was based on an ideal order, a vision of justice, something fundamentally static which, once achieved, is to be preserved. But that is the last thing they want, for they are always progressing toward something new. Or take laws protecting women workers. At one time these were desired by liberals, and rightly so. Indeed, Catholics could and often did support the same measures. (See *Quadragesimo Anno*, nos. 25–28.) But with a difference. Catholics supported them because we knew they were a step in the right direction, in the direction of a just society. And if you had asked an informed Catholic he could have given you an outline of the kind of society and the kind of economy the Church was calling for. But not the liberal. At one time he supported laws protecting women workers, then, some decades later, he wishes to abolish them because they stand in the way of his newly-discovered principle that there are no important differences between the sexes and special legislation for women workers is in fact a form of discrimination against women or even a kind of oppression.

At one time liberals were pretty much absolutists with regard to free speech. Now, of course, it's the opposite, and the most advanced liberals are leading the fight to condemn or restrict speech which is seen as harmful to certain minority groups. Liberalism is always discovering something new that we need to be liberated from. In the United States the civil rights struggle is paradigmatic for liberals. And of course, it was an entirely just struggle, one that should not have been necessary even to fight, for the revival of slavery and the slave trade, and in particular the division of humanity into "races" based chiefly on skin color was utterly contrary to Catholic teaching. So naturally the civil rights movement was in accord with Catholic principles.

And liberals of the time also supported it, often courageously. But now the principles of equality and brotherhood that at the time were thought to be the goal of the fight are increasingly rejected by advanced liberalism, for once again liberals have discovered a hitherto unknown principle, the supposed oppressive hegemony of European-descended peoples — those who are stupidly known as *whites* — and hence it calls not for brotherhood but for separation or even for hostility. At one time liberals rejected out of hand the notion that an individual could be condemned simply because he was part of a particular group; now they are fast returning to such notions. So, to sum up, liberalism has no goal; the restraints which it seeks to be freed from are always changing and can even contradict what liberals wanted yesterday. No one knows what it will demand tomorrow.

Above I said that American conservatism is part of liberalism, for, strangely enough, people can and do embrace the liberalism of a century ago or a decade ago, so that at any point in time there are different types of liberals in existence. But it is of the movement as a whole that I am speaking here, and to which what I have said applies most fully.

But while liberalism is wrong, it's important to note that the critics of liberalism are diverse, and that there are some very strange ideologies among these critics. We should eschew the maxim that the enemy of my enemy is necessarily my friend. Just because someone is a critic of liberalism does not mean that he is an ally. The Church, as someone has said, is fighting on every front at the same time.

This is not to say that Catholics can't make temporary alliances with the most various sorts of groups for specific ends. You might recall that some time ago the Vatican worked with Muslim countries at the United Nations to defeat some noxious proposals on the family that were being advanced at some UN conferences. The problem occurs when we start thinking that certain groups are permanent and natural allies. If they are not Catholic, then it's obvious that we disagree with them on some important and vital points, points which we can't ignore just because we're in the midst of some political battle or because we consider some other group as more hostile. In fact, we've got to keep in mind that the maxim, *The enemy of my enemy is my friend*, is false, and leads Catholics to make fatal alliances with groups of one sort or another that, if not actually hostile to us, at least tend to discredit us and make our apostolic work so much harder in the long run. Also, it's very hard to judge long-term results, so instead we look to merely short-term results. A certain movement or group might seem less of a threat in the near-term, but if its fundamental principles are not Catholic, we cannot regard it as a natural or permanent ally.

Liberty is perhaps one of the most confusing and misunderstood terms in the English language. What is the Catholic view of liberty?

Leo XIII devoted an entire encyclical to this question, *Libertas* of June 1888. First he distinguishes what he calls "natural liberty," the ability of rational creatures to choose freely among various goods.

> Considered as to its nature, it is the faculty of choosing means fitted for the end proposed, for he is master of his actions who can choose one thing out of many. Now, since everything chosen as a means is viewed as good or useful, and since good, as such, is the proper object of our desire, it follows that freedom of choice is a property of the will, or, rather, is identical with the will in so far as it has in its action the faculty of choice. (no. 5)

Then, with regard to political liberty, he wrote,

> Therefore, the true liberty of human society does not consist in every man doing what he pleases, for this would simply end in turmoil and confusion, and bring on the overthrow of the State; but rather in this, that through the injunctions of the civil law all may more easily conform to the prescriptions of the eternal law. Likewise, the liberty of those who are in authority does not consist in the power to lay unreasonable and capricious commands upon their subjects, which would equally be criminal and would lead to the ruin of the commonwealth; but the binding force of human laws is in this, that they are to be regarded as applications of the eternal law, and incapable of sanctioning anything which is not contained in the eternal law, as in the principle of all law. Thus, St. Augustine most wisely says: "I think that you can see, at the same time, that there is nothing just and lawful in that temporal law, unless what men have gathered from this eternal law." If, then, by anyone in authority, something be sanctioned out of conformity with the principles of right reason, and consequently hurtful to the commonwealth, such an enactment can have no binding force of law, as being no rule of justice, but certain to lead men away from that good which is the very end of civil society. (no. 10)

Although there is much more in the encyclical, I think these two passages sum up his and the Church's doctrine. Mankind has by nature the ability to choose among goods. But very often men choose wrongly, they choose what, considered in all their aspects and context, are not really goods. For example, pleasure considered in itself is a good, but when it's divorced from its place in the hierarchy of means and ends it loses the character of being a good. If I eat five pieces of cake for dessert because it tastes so good, the pleasure of eating loses its real character of goodness when I get a stomach ache or gain excessive weight.

As to political liberty, as Leo points out, this is subordinate to just civil law. The notion of freedom as the highest political good, which is common in the United States among persons of the most diverse views, is not a sound political maxim, but is one of the notes of a Protestant cultural or political outlook. Sometimes this has been stated explicitly by Protestants or those of Protestant culture.

> In response to criticism of his 1965 lecture, "Church and State," prominent Canadian historian Arthur Lower stated: "The only point I try to make... is that the individual's right to decide for himself, not only in religion, but in all other spheres, is the founding principle of Protestantism. The very essence of Catholicism, on the other hand, is the necessity of the individual's submitting to authority," adding that "[t]here is still a 'burning at the stake' waiting for the disobedient Catholic, it must be remembered — in the form... of excommunication." Lower went on to outline how the distinctly Protestant values of individualism and self-government in church and state were the defining characteristics of modern industrial society.[2]

I think it's obvious that this notion of freedom is pretty widespread in the United States, indeed that it is one of the fundamental elements of our national cultural personality.

---

2   Quoted in Kevin Anderson, *Anti-Catholicism and English Canadian Nationalism*, Thesis Submitted to the School of Graduate Studies, McMaster University, 2013, p. 1.

And it arose from Protestantism, quite naturally. But it's also been assimilated by most American Catholics of both ideological camps. But the incompatibility of this with genuine Catholicism should be clear to anyone.

There seems to be an ongoing debate today on liberalism as found through various publications both print and online. Do you think this debate has been fruitful?

I have not always followed this debate closely, so I am giving merely my impressions here. But my impression is that this discussion is too often perceived and framed as a discussion or debate among conservatives, between libertarians and other types of conservatives. But this is fundamentally wrong and confused. Unless the critique of liberalism is a critique of the entire liberal tradition, including what we call conservatism in the United States, it is of little importance, for it shows that the participants have not understood what liberalism really is. But if we accept the critique of liberalism that Cardinal Billot made, and that I have made myself, we get beyond the categories of conservative and liberal as they are used today. Liberalism does have a useful meaning, in the sense that Cardinal Billot understands and dissects it, but conservative is a hopelessly confused and confusing term and should be abandoned. It doesn't aid our thinking, it makes it more difficult to sort out political traditions and ideas. In fact, it's almost meaningless outside of a particular and specific historical context.

If we undertake a critique of liberalism, then, we are stepping outside the entire liberal tradition, a tradition that in the English-speaking world bases itself almost entirely on the thought of John Locke. Those who seriously undertake this critique are, of course, not liberals, but neither does the term conservative apply to them in any sensible manner. If we want to use the term *conservative*, then we should apply it in a particular concrete historical instance to mean those who want to conserve something, and obviously this something can differ considerably, so at one time or place a conservative could be someone who wants to conserve monarchy, at another time socialism, and so on. To use the word as if it meant some ideology which exists independently of such concrete circumstances seems to me misleading. Add to this that the term as used in the U. S. most often denotes a political stance which, historically speaking, is anything but conservative, that is, that champions one of the most destructive and transformative ideologies the world has ever known, liberal capitalism. Christopher Dawson noted this in the following,

> The United States achieved their independence in the heyday of the European Enlightenment, and this ideology of the Enlightenment was the foundation of their national existence. The peoples of Europe, in spite of their revolutions, were committed to the past and to their separate national traditions. But Americans were committed to the future. They saw the Revolution as the dawn of a new age and a new civilization which was destined to be the civilization of a new world, and consequently the principles of the Constitution and the Declaration of Independence were not transitory and fallible opinions but absolute truths which no citizen could question and which were to remain the firm foundations of the American way of life.[3]

From this arose a certain confusion, for this commitment to the future that Americans had became the national ideology, and those who defend this essentially revolutionary

---

3   Christopher Dawson, *The Crisis of Western Education* (New York: Sheed & Ward, c. 1961), p. 182.

political stance label themselves as conservatives, since they want to conserve the only tradition they know, and which is "the foundation of their national existence" as a polity. But any meaningful debate about liberalism in the United States must recognize this fact, must begin in fact with a critique of the Lockean liberal tradition which colors the thinking of the overwhelming majority of American citizens.

You have written extensively on the influence of John Locke on the founding of the United States. Could you perhaps summarize how he influenced the founders? Out of all the thinkers why was John Locke chosen to have such a key role in the philosophical underpinnings of the United States?

Locke's thought caught on since already the English had moved away from the medieval conception of a monarch who had a care for the well-being of his people to a notion of government as simply keeping the peace and upholding rights, and usually the rights of the rich and powerful. John Locke provided an intellectual justification for this understanding of government, a simple but powerful framework by which the purposes and functions of government could be evaluated. His ideas were already "in the air," so to speak, at least by the mid-eighteenth century, so it was natural that the American founders were heavily influenced by them and made use of them. They had been brought up on them. You can see his influence everywhere, for example, in our Declaration of Independence, in the Virginia Statute on Religious Liberty, which Thomas Jefferson considered as one of his greatest achievements, in fact as the background of the political thinking of that entire founding generation.

5
Politics

In the United States, for all practical purposes, there is a two-party system. Can a Catholic in good conscience work within this system? How does a Catholic get involved in politics in order to effect change? Or is the system so fundamentally flawed that it does not matter what the individual does?

There are probably nooks and crannies, as it were, in both major parties in which a Catholic can honesty operate, but I think they are few and far between, and becoming less and less so. Each party is committed to so many things that a Catholic can hardly accept with a clear conscience, and each party expects that its members who hold elective office will conform to the party platform. And right now politics seems especially corrupt and corrupting, as well. At the local level there is doubtless some good that can be done by a sincere Catholic — but only if he is both savvy enough to see the temptations that so often abound for him and virtuous enough to resist them. A friend of mine very recently became a village councilor in a small village, and I expect he's likely to be able to do a considerable amount of good in that position. I think this is one of the "nooks and crannies" where an honest Catholic can do some good. But note that it's a non-partisan office, as are local offices in many places.

Although we can't expect much electoral success, and certainly not right now, I would recommend that Catholics get involved in the American Solidarity party, a political party that is by and large in agreement with Catholic teaching across the board. To be sure, the ASP is not perfect, even in its principles and platform, but it's the nearest thing to a Christian Democratic party we are likely to see in the U. S.

for a long, long time. Its importance, however, in my view is more as a witness than as having a realistic hope for achieving political power. And given the corruption of our culture, I'm far from sure that an ASP administration — if there ever were one — could itself resist the manifold temptations that abound for those in public office.

What about the argument that we must vote for the political candidate who will do the least amount of harm — the 'lesser of two evils' argument? Is that an option? Should it be up to an individual's conscience to decide whom to vote for?

There might be times when it makes sense to vote for the lesser of two evils. But to do so over and over again when there is a better way, makes no sense to me. Catholics are a large enough segment of the population so that if enough of us demanded a platform reasonably in conformity with the range of Catholic socio-economic and moral teaching, then it's possible some major candidate would listen to us and offer us something conformable to that. But of course, to get enough Catholics to do so, those who largely form Catholic opinion, our clergy and our media, would have to give us guidance along those lines, and right now that's not happening. In fact, to the extent we are given guidance, it's the "lesser of two evils" option that we're exhorted to go with.

With regard to your second question — Should it be up to the individual's conscience to decide whom to vote for? — in general I would say yes, though I know that in the past in certain countries Catholics were told to vote or not to vote for certain political parties. And I imagine that that was the case in the U. S. also, say with regard to Communist or Socialist parties. But regardless of whether that was a good idea or not, it's not something that's likely to happen again soon. So even though an individual voter will have to decide for himself, there is a tremendous field for educational work in this regard. I'm thinking not only of the pulpit, but especially of Catholic media. If the Catholic media of all types embraced a really Catholic approach to social and economic questions, they could do a huge amount of good in forming Catholic public opinion and guiding Catholics in their choices as voters, and not just as voters, but as consumers, and as participants in all aspects of economic and social and cultural life.

In terms of making natural allies — and this in no way is meant to diminish some of the individual successes they have achieved — do you think the pro-life movement which encompasses a wide-range of groups from Catholic to Protestants is an example of an alliance to which Catholics should be cautious of?

Since it's an alliance which has a specific and certainly legitimate goal, I wouldn't put it among the alliances I spoke of above. Of course, Catholics involved in the right-to-life movement have to make sure that they don't start thinking that common action to fight abortion is more important than the doctrinal differences we have with Protestants. Many Christians, both Catholic and Protestant, believe that something they call *conservative* Christianity, by which they mean a Christianity that takes what is called in the U. S. a conservative position on certain currently-debated moral questions — chiefly abortion and homosexuality and so-called gender issues — that this is a permanent or semi-permanent entity or alliance, an entity which crosses confessional lines and makes our formal doctrinal commitments unimportant in contrast with our shared moral positions. The former Catholic, Rod Dreher, represents this point of view, for he's stated explicitly that the doctrinal differences that Christians have are comparatively unimportant in the face of the moral or political threats we confront. I think this point of view is profoundly wrong, in fact, backwards, since it's our moral positions that are grounded upon our doctrines, not the other way around.

For Catholics, and for men of good will, how does one conceptually break the mold of thinking in terms of party politics?

Party politics, at least as they exist today—and I think this is true in every country, or nearly every—are a reflection of our left/right thinking. That is the root of the problem. The division of parties and political opinion along the lines of left/right came from the seating of delegates to the French national assembly after the French revolution. It was a particular manifestation of political opinions for one place and time. The absurdity of it is shown in that groups who are classified, say, as on the Right might hold rather diverse opinions on a multitude of points, on economics, in particular, but on other matters as well. I wrote some years ago, "Some time ago I saw an amusing description of the gathering known as the Philadelphia Society, a meeting that takes place every year in that Pennsylvania city. The writer called it a place for anyone who considers himself a conservative, from those who want to sell off public parks to the highest bidder to those who yearn for a restoration of the Hapsburg monarchy."

Now the Hapsburg monarchy was not a libertarian or small government regime. So how can we possibly classify as conservatives or on the Right both those who support small government, i.e., a government that is limited to enforcing law and order and has no concern for promoting the common good or virtue—who are in fact classical liberals or libertarians—with those who want to restore the old European monarchical order, an order which most definitely *was* concerned with promoting the common good and virtue? By what logic are both of these positions called conservative? By no logic, as far as I can see.

The model taken from the seating in the French assembly assumes that one can place persons and positions on a linear spectrum. But where do you place someone who wants to make abortion illegal but who at the same time thinks that capitalism rarely or never works to promote justice? This silly linear spectrum can't deal with this. And as a result of this way of thinking, someone, say, who upholds the Church's teaching on marriage is classified as a *conservative*, even though that same person, if he is faithful to the Church's social teachings, will hardly be an advocate of free-market policies.

Moreover, when we look at the policies which are generally associated in the United States with liberalism or conservatism, they have no coherence. Why, for example, should someone who supports labor unions also support abortion? There is no logical connection between these two policies. Or with the opposite policies either.

On certain websites, say, *The American Conservative*, you will see commenters arguing about what conservatism is. Do or must conservatives support libertarian economic policies? Do they or must they support an active or bellicose foreign policy, or perhaps the opposite? It becomes clear that the mere term, the word itself, is as important to some people as the actual policies they espouse. Until we manage to get people to stop thinking in terms of Left/Right, liberal/conservative, we will not be able to break down their blind adherence to our current party politics.

Some writers have suggested a four-fold division of political opinions, a marked improvement over our Left/Right spectrum, even though still not perfect. The chart below is one version of this schema.

Seeing the World with Catholic Eyes

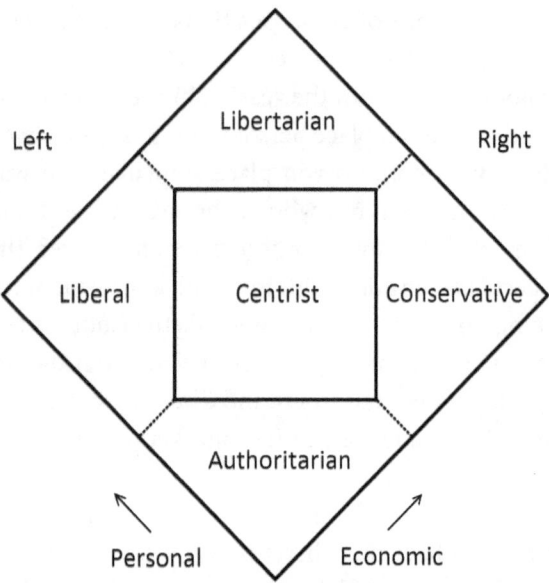

(Chart created by David Nolan and originally published in 1971 in an article,"Classifying and Analyzing Politico-Economic Systems" in the January 1971 issue of *The Individualist*.)

Wikipedia summarizes this approach as follows:

> According to Nolan, since most government activity (or government control) occurs in these two major areas, political positions can be defined by how much government control a person or political party favors in these two areas. The extremes are no government at all in either area (anarchism) or total or near-total government control of everything (various forms of totalitarianism). Most political philosophies fall somewhere in between. In broad terms:
>
> Those on the right, including American conservatives, tend to favor more freedom in economic matters (example: a free market), but more

government intervention in personal matters (example: drug laws).

Those on the left, including American liberals, tend to favor more freedom in personal matters (example: no military draft), but more government activism or control in economics (example: a government-mandated minimum wage).

Libertarians favor both personal and economic freedom and oppose most (or all) government intervention in both areas. Like conservatives, libertarians believe in free markets. Like liberals, libertarians believe in personal freedom.

Authoritarians favor a lot of government control in both the personal and economic areas. Different versions of the chart as well as Nolan's original chart use terms such as "totalitarian", "statist", "communitarian" or "populist" to label this corner of the chart. (https://en.wikipedia.org/wiki/Nolan_Chart)

The last position here, whether labeled as authoritarian or communitarian, is unfortunately not widely held or even widely known in the United States, but perhaps the current debates about (classical) liberalism could help people see that it is a viable option and one that happens to be largely in accord with the Church's own teaching.

And of course, there can be important differences in how policies are actually applied. Thus a Catholic will tend to favor economic regulation being carried out by lower bodies, the guilds or occupational groups that I mentioned before, while a communist or fascist would favor direct economic regulation by the state. Clearly these differences are important.

Another point of criticism of this four-fold approach is that it fails to distinguish the philosophies that underlie political opinions. Different people could take the same or a similar position on an issue or set of issues and yet have very divergent political philosophies or philosophical anthropologies. Pius XI gives a very good example of this when he comments on the Italian Fascist economy in *Quadragesimo Anno* (nos. 91-5). He notes how the Fascist idea of the occupational group — or *corporation*, as in corporatist state — differs from a Catholic one, despite the superficial similarities they shared. For the Fascist, the *corporation* was to be a government entity or agency, not a true society of those working in the same trade or business. The Fascists wanted to impose occupational order from the top down, while Pius wished it to arise from the actual activities of employers and workers themselves, with of course general support by the government. That, by the way, was what John Paul II meant in a much misunderstood phrase in *Centesimus Annus* (no. 43): "The Church has no models to present; models that are real and truly effective can only arise within the framework of different historical situations, through the efforts of all those who responsibly confront concrete problems in all their social, economic, political and cultural aspects, as these interact with one another." Economies and cultures as a whole differ so much across time and place that a top-down approach to bringing order and justice into an economy is not the right way to go.

So although the Fascist corporation and the Catholic occupational group certainly share certain features and both could be defined as organizations of all those working in the same trade or industry, the spirit that animated each would differ considerably. That is why Pius is his later encyclical, *Divini Redemptoris*, was careful to call for "a sane corporative system which respects the proper hierarchic structure of society" (no. 32), instead of Mussolini's overly bureaucratic system. Moreover, I remind the reader what I said before about liberalism. Even when its goals approximate those of

Catholic social doctrine, it is animated by its desire to throw off any and all restraints on human conduct, not on a vision of what a just social order would be like.

6
Americanism

In Pope Leo XIII's letter, Testem Benevolentiae Nostrae, *"Americanism" is condemned as the exaltation of the active virtues over the passive ones. Is there a different sense to "Americanism" as the type of role the United States has taken in world affairs, both ecclesiastically and politically?*

Although it might seem that they are different things, I think that in many ways Americanism as specified by Leo XIII is responsible for the things you mention, for the role the U. S. has taken—or tried to take—both in the Church and the world. Although Catholics in the United States long claimed absolute loyalty to the Church's faith and the Holy See, for a long time there has been an undercurrent—or perhaps more than an undercurrent—of the idea that this country really is a new type of thing in human history, not merely a configuration of old ideas such as republicanism, representative government, and so on, but a new order of the ages, as the Great Seal of the United States proclaims. And so the "virtues" associated with the American character, the active or natural virtues, as they have been sometimes called, became the new standard by which human behavior must be judged. Pope Leo discussed this in the following words,

> This overesteem of natural virtue finds a method of expression in assuming to divide all virtues in active and passive, and it is alleged that whereas passive virtues found better place in past times, our age is to be characterized by the active.

Do we not see more than a hint of this condemned idea in these words of Dr. Benjamin Rush, one of the signers of the Declaration of Independence, in his essay, "Observations Upon the Study of the Latin and Greek Languages"?

> We occupy a new country. Our principal business should be to explore and apply its resources, all of which press us to enterprize and haste. Under these circumstances, to spend four or five years in learning two dead languages, is to turn our backs upon a gold mine, in order to amuse ourselves in catching butterflies.

Americans have never been inclined to turn their backs upon a gold mine — indeed education, and all of life, as merely a project for moneymaking has been one of the constants of the American character. And in rejecting or setting aside the wisdom of our civilization — "two dead languages" — do we not come close to what Leo XIII described as "the assumed right to hold whatever opinions one pleases upon any subject and to set them forth in print to the world..."? And from this it is merely another step to the "suspicion that there are among you some who conceive and would have the Church in America to be different from what it is in the rest of the world...."

But if the United States *is* different, if we really are exceptional, are we not entitled to impose our ideas of life upon the rest of mankind, upon those Calvin Coolidge described in his inaugural address as the "less favored peoples" of the world? After all, are we not simply doing them a favor to extend principles which are not merely our own, but destined for the entire human race? As Woodrow Wilson said in his second inaugural address in 1917,

> We shall be the more American if we but remain true to the principles in which we have been bred. They are not the principles of a province or of a single continent. We have known and boasted all

along that they were the principles of a liberated mankind.

One could multiply to a great extent such expressions of the idea that the principles which Americans claim underlie this country are in fact universal, are meant for mankind as a whole, that they are held in trust, as it were, for the rest of the world by the United States. Daniel Webster, in an oration delivered in August 1826, had stated this idea in the following words:

> It cannot be denied, but by those who would dispute against the sun, that with America, and in America, a new era commences in human affairs. This era is distinguished by free representative governments, by entire religious liberty, by improved systems of national intercourse, by a newly awakened and an unconquerable spirit of free inquiry, and by a diffusion of knowledge through the community, such as has been before altogether unknown and unheard of. America ... is inseparably connected, fast bound up, in fortune and by fate, with these great interests.... Let us contemplate, then, this connection, which binds the prosperity of others to our own; and let us manfully discharge all the duties which it imposes. If we cherish the virtues and the principles of our fathers, Heaven will assist us to carry on the work of human liberty and human happiness.

Carrying on "the work of human liberty and human happiness" has meant at times trying to impose our own way of life on other nations. In Puerto Rico, for example, after we seized that island as a spoil of the Spanish-American War, we tried to Americanize the population, for a time insisting that all public education be conducted in English, even though almost all students and most teachers had no knowledge of that language. And of course, more recently we have seen the debacle of trying to impose democracy in the Middle East. So although Pope Leo was focused on other points, they are certainly related to the role the U. S. has played in our own hemisphere, and especially since World War II, throughout the world.

This ideology of American exceptionalism is practically an article of faith in many circles, and to question it marks one as unpatriotic. One can find this idea reiterated over and over again, e.g., in this recent article by Victor Davis Hanson on *National Review* online, "Thoughts on the 1776 Commission and Its Report."

> But any fair critic can see that the [1776 Commission] report's unifying message is that we are a people blessed with a singular government and history, that self-critique and moral improvement are innate to the American Founding and spirit, and that America never had to be perfect to be both good and far better than the alternatives.

I find such language incredible. It's surely silly to claim that any one nation is the greatest. One nation is better at one thing, another at another thing. Americans who insist that we are exceptional in the sense of being the best, assume a set of criteria that is arbitrary and more than questionable, usually centered around the notion of freedom or economic growth or technology. They rarely ask themselves if perhaps the nations with the fewest abortions or divorces, or the least poverty or the greatest literature or music are not in fact the greatest.

There is one further step in this Americanism that I should mention. This is the notion that the United States is not essentially a nation, a place, even a place that embodies universal principles destined for everyone. This is the notion that we are primarily a notion, that is an idea. George H. W. Bush said in his State of the Union Message in January 1990,

> America — not just the nation — but an idea, alive in the minds of people everywhere. As this new world takes shape, America stands at the center of a widening circle of freedom today, tomorrow and into the next century.

America becomes here primarily an idea, and the actual place is chiefly important as somewhere for this idea to be realized. This is not only a very odd understanding of what it means to be a country, but, as I said, dangerous, and in certain of its manifestations, bordering on the sacrilegious, with absurd notions about the quasi-divine origins of the Constitution, and so on.

America as an "idea" to be imposed reminds me of what Steven Mintz says in his book, Moralists & Modernizers: America's Pre-Civil War Reformers: *"The notion that the American Revolution inaugurated a new epoch in human history, a new era of virtue, justice, equality, and possibility, was widely shared by late-eighteenth-century and early nineteenth-century Americans . . . Many secular Americans also believed that the United States was the New Israel, destined to lead the world to universal peace and prosperity" (p. 16). If this is such an ingrained principle in the American psyche, if that follows from this passage, how can the Catholic steer clear of this sort of messianic approach to America's role in the world?*

It should be obvious to a Catholic that there's something very wrong with this American messianism, but unfortunately, since at least the Americanist movement of the late nineteenth century, and probably even well before that, there were plenty of Catholics who saw nothing wrong with this secular vision of America as a new Israel. In order to counteract it, Catholics have to be explicitly taught that it's wrong and why it's wrong. But for that to happen, priests and Catholic school teachers must understand that, and before that, their own teachers, those who form seminarians and teach Catholic university students, must grasp this. I don't see this happening anytime soon.

Can one be a "patriot" and still criticize one's nation? How does one show a true love for one's country?

Well, certainly. Nothing on this earth is perfect, and we can hardly be expected to uncritically support — or fail to criticize — our country just because it is ours and because we do owe it a certain loyalty and love. This is implied in my answer to your last question. But a more complete answer must begin with a definition of patriotism. In his book, *The Four Loves*, C. S. Lewis talks about the four varieties of love, affection, friendship, eros and charity. Affection is the kind of love one has for people simply because they have been placed near one in life, for our family and relatives, for example. But we can also have affection for a place, for our neighborhood, our city or town, and for our country. We love it simply because it is our own, because we feel comfortable with its customs and ways of doing things, and, as we become older and conscious of our duties and of the goods that we have received, we become aware of the benefits that we have received from these places, for example, our education. We love our country, then, because she is ours and because she has given us certain benefits. But just as most of us would be willing to admit that our families are not perfect and even deserve criticism at times, so we must be willing to do the same with our countries. There is nothing against patriotism here, it is simply common sense.

7
Culture

You have often spoken of the role of culture in shaping a people. How would you define culture and how is it important in terms of the exercise of the Catholic Faith?

In 1871 Edward Tylor, an English anthropologist, offered the first coherent definition of the anthropological meaning of culture in the English-speaking world. He wrote that culture is "that complex whole which includes knowledge, beliefs, arts, morals, law, customs, and any other capabilities and habits acquired by man as a member of society."[1]

Although this concept was clarified and articulated only in the nineteenth century, it is much much older. In the very first chapter of his *Gallic Wars* Julius Caesar discusses the three chief population groups inhabiting Gaul, and says that *"lingua, institutis, legibus inter se differunt,"* that is, they differ among themselves in language, customs and laws. Obviously, this is to say what Tylor said, without using the term culture.

This usage of culture is in contrast to an older meaning, perhaps best expressed by Matthew Arnold only a few years before Tylor wrote. For Arnold culture is "a pursuit of our total perfection by means of getting to know, on all the matters which most concern us, the best which has been thought and said in the world."[2] This usage of the word is akin to the common understanding of culture as the fine arts, great literature and so on.

---

1 *Primitive Culture: Researches into the Development of Mythology, Philosophy, Religion, Language, Art, and Custom*, London, 1871, chapter 1.
2 *Culture and Anarchy*, Preface.

Both usages can be defended and can be useful, and both still coexist side by side. But Catholic and other Christian writers, notably Christopher Dawson, Hilaire Belloc, and the Anglican T. S. Eliot, have made very fruitful use of the term culture in its anthropological sense. The reason for this fruitful usage on the part of Catholics is that the term culture allows one to succinctly summarize the effect of Catholic faith and practice on individuals and societies. This was well put by the Jesuit, Fr. George Bull, in an article in the journal *Thought*.[3]

> In recent years, Catholics have become increasingly conscious of the clash between Catholicism as a general culture, and the culture of the world around them. The work of men like Belloc, Maritain, Christopher Dawson and others, has shown that we differ not in religion alone, but in the whole realm of unspoken and spontaneous things, which color even our daily routine.

And even before Fr. Bull wrote, Belloc could use that concept of "Catholicism as a general culture," in his seminal essay, "The Two Cultures of the West," (in *Essays of a Catholic*). Belloc wrote,

> There is a Protestant culture and a Catholic culture. The difference between these two is the main difference dividing one sort of European from another. The boundary between the Catholic and Protestant cultures is the great line of cleavage, compared with which all others are secondary.

Using this concept we can examine the effects of Catholic belief on individuals, and especially on societies, on a

---

3 "The Function of the Catholic Graduate School," *Thought*, vol. 13, issue 3, September 1938.

society's institutions, laws, customs, etc. Even prior to when Dawson and Belloc wrote, in the nineteenth century, the Spanish priest and philosopher, Jaime Balmes, had attempted something of the same with his *Protestantism and Catholicity Compared in Their Effects on the Civilization of Europe*. And Cardinal Newman speaks of the Catholic folk customs of Italy and how different the outlook was there, as well as in medieval Europe, from Protestant England. And this should be clear even today with the Faith in decline everywhere; the differences between nations of historic Catholic cultures from those with historic Protestant cultures are pretty obvious, sometimes in surprising ways. But in the United States most Catholics have adopted, to one degree or another, important aspects of a Protestant cultural outlook, so I think there is resistance to accepting, or even understanding, the notion of "Catholicism as a general culture." It would necessitate abandoning too many of our political and economic ideas that we have taken over from the surrounding Protestant culture.

Could you perhaps give a few examples of the way these cultural differences manifest themselves concretely?

I wrote about this in the May 2020 *New Oxford Review*.

> But what are the elements of this [American cultural] creed which are so at odds with the Catholic faith and with the Catholic approach to thought and life, and which continue to shape our culture even as it has ceased to hold Protestant religious doctrines? I think that the elements of the American national outlook concern two areas chiefly. The first might be called philosophical or better epistemological, for it concerns human knowledge and its acquisition, while the second concerns the social order. With regard to the first, American

thought vacillates between the extremes of faith, conceived in a purely fideistic or fiduciary manner, and a reductionist scientific or empiricist approach to knowledge. Americans understand knowledge which has an immediate practical end, technological or financial, for example; they also understand, even if increasingly they reject, religious faith conceived as a simple act of trust motivated by the emotions or the will. But what they do not understand nor do they see the value of, is rational knowledge, such as philosophy, which is not based on the methods of the natural sciences, but which nevertheless claims for itself the status of knowledge....

Christopher Dawson, in a 1960 lecture delivered at the University of St. Thomas in Houston, commented on this American view in these words:

Thus American religion was detached from the objective world which was the domain of business and politics and focused on the subjective world of religious feeling—above all the intense experience of religious conversion. This, I believe, has left a permanent mark on the American mind, so that, as several Americans have remarked to me, they find some difficulty in relating the two concepts of religion and civilization since these seem to belong to two quite distinct orders of existence....

From this results both the tendency to value education as merely a means to moneymaking and advancement in life, as well as the often lamented overspecialization of American education and American intellectual life as a whole. The value of specialized knowledge is obvious: it tends to pay; general knowledge does not. Thus the complaint of Theodore Maynard, "In no other country in the world can first-rate doctors and lawyers be encountered who know nothing outside of their own profession. Culture, not having a cash value, is disesteemed."[4]

The second fundamental anti-Catholic element in American thought concerns, as I remarked, the social order. Here it is individualism, a trait widely noted in the American character, including a suspicion of or even hostility toward social authority, toward hierarchy, toward any restraints on one's conduct originating outside of one's self, whether in the religious or political spheres. With regard to religion, it is most obvious among Evangelical Protestants, who are prone to start a new religious denomination at the drop of a hat, rather than submit to decisions they might disagree with. Sadly, this attitude has affected Catholics in the United States as well, as I suggested when we spoke about Americanism before.

In addition to these aspects, which I regard as fundamental, these cultural differences manifest themselves in many areas, including our attitudes toward leisure and work, food, sex and the body, marriage and many other areas.

---

[4] *The Story of American Catholicism* (New York: Macmillan, 1941), p. 586.

8
Living as Catholics in the Modern World

Many immigrants left Europe (and elsewhere) to make a new living in the United States (and Canada) which was called the 'land of opportunity.' How would you explain why so many left Europe to live in the U. S. if its economy was so fundamentally flawed? What was so desirous that they would leave their history, culture, communities behind?

First, a point that's often overlooked by those of us in North America. There was not only considerable immigration to the U. S. and Canada, but to Latin America as well, especially, I think, to Argentina and Brazil, but to other countries also. This immigration is often totally unknown or ignored, as if Europeans looked longingly at the United States as the realization of the age-long wishes of humanity. In truth, I think the main thing that drove so many people here was economic need, more than economic opportunity or the desire to share in the American system or way of life. That is, the poverty of so many in Europe. It was generally from countries with the greatest number of poor, the widest conditions of poverty, from which the most immigrants came. If one was unable to provide for one's family at home, then political and cultural questions, and even the character of the U. S. economy, became of secondary importance. Moreover, we should not forget the fact that many immigrants came here with the intention of staying only temporarily and then returning. And many did return. St. Pio's father, that is Padre Pio's father, came here and worked and then returned to Italy.

Some immigrants, I'm sure, did see the U. S. as a land of opportunity. They were already imbued with the spirit of American capitalism and saw this land as a place where they could realize their dreams of riches. But these were the minority, I think.

A term that is often used to describe the intellectual and moral climate associated with the contemporary world is "modernity." Can you trace the origins of "modernity" and offer a definition of this term?

There have been many attempts to trace the origins of modernity and to specify what exactly is unique about it. More than one author has said, and I think this is correct, that its remote origins go back to nominalism, the philosophical doctrine which became so popular in the later Middle Ages and undermined so much of theology. Nominalism essentially made God unknowable by reason. Henceforth it was only by an appeal to revelation that his nature and commandments could be known. The resemblance to Protestantism should be apparent here.

It seems to me that modernity in the sense we are discussing it here became fully established as a social order when religious truth became a purely private matter, when there was no longer an official or semi-official religion for society. This must have had in the long run an immense impact on the thinking of ordinary people, to be told, in essence, that now you're responsible for religious truth, no longer is it a community matter, something that we all hold together. We take this view for granted today, but I think it was probably one of the most momentous changes in human history.

In Europe up to almost the end of the eighteenth century society did have such an official or semi-official religion. Ironically, even the French Revolutionaries sought to perpetuate such a state of things; their cult of reason was nothing more than an official religion imposed — violently imposed in fact — on French society. The United States, on the other hand, was the first, certainly the first important nation, to state on a national level that the political community as such had no connection with religion, that it was a private matter. Although it is true that some of the individual states had religious establishments even up to the 1830s, these were obviously holdovers from the past, and in contrast with the federal government's growing power, both political and cultural, of increasingly little significance.

A few years ago, Rod Dreher wrote about the "Benedict Option" which is described on the American Conservative *site[1] as referring "to Christians in the contemporary West who cease to identify the continuation of civility and moral community with the maintenance of American empire, and who therefore are keen to construct local forms of community as loci of Christian resistance against what the empire represents. Put less grandly, the Benedict Option — or "Ben Op" — is an umbrella term for Christians who accept MacIntyre's critique of modernity, and who also recognize that forming Christians who live out Christianity according to Great Tradition requires embedding within communities and institutions dedicated to that formation." In your view, is this a good model to pursue?*

You ask if this is a good model for *Christians* "to pursue." This echoes Dreher himself, whose intended audience consists of "conservative Christians." In my review of this book in the September 2017 *New Oxford Review*, I noted that Dreher "displays a curious lack of concern about basic theological distinctions." That is, he writes for what he calls "conservative Christians," be they Protestant, Catholic or Orthodox, Christians who more or less agree on currently controverted

---

[1] See: https://www.theamericanconservative.com/dreher/benedict-option-faq/

questions such as abortion, homosexual conduct, transgenderism, etc. This means more to him than fundamental theological principles about the Fall, redemption, grace, the Church, the sacraments, and so on. I think he has it exactly backwards. Morality proceeds from doctrine, not the other way around. So if you ask me what I think about "Christians" in general implementing something like the "Benedict option," I have to reply that I'm not particularly interested in how non-Catholic Christians implement this or anything else. If we see our society in grave disorder, part of that disorder is due precisely to Protestantism, so they and their projects are not part of the solution; rather the contrary. For instance, if in the United States one of the causes of many of our troubles lies in an individualism that refuses to accept authority, it is chiefly because of Protestantism that this individualism is such a powerful cultural force. And as Benedict XVI pointed out in his Regensburg address, it is Protestants, as much as Muslims, who have sought to separate God from reason, to the great detriment of theological thinking.

So, to refine your question, do I think something like the Benedict option is good for *Catholics*? My answer is, yes, for some Catholics. But there are many ways to engage and evangelize the culture, and not everyone has the same vocation or the same gifts. In my review of Dreher's book that I mentioned, I wrote, "Catholics must seek to discern how God wishes each of us to respond to the civilizational crisis we now face. For some people, withdrawal into intentional rural communities is the answer; for others, it is selective engagement with various cultural or even political organs and institutions; for others, there are doubtless different tactics." I realize that Dreher himself does not suggest only one single approach. So the book can be a good starting point for discussions of how to live as Catholics today, but we should avoid making it of more significance than it is.

How would you view the role of the mass media in today's discourse on religion and politics? Is it fair to say that the mass media has had an increasingly strong role in forming or de-forming minds for that?

Based on my limited consumption of mass media—I don't watch television and rarely listen to radio and try to be selective about internet use, I'd say that the media has little understanding of religion and pretty much subsumes it into its political analyses, which themselves are pretty shallow. But doubtless many people, including most Catholics, have their ideas shaped by the media's understanding of things.

Our society is secular, yes, obviously. But it's a peculiar kind of secularism, a post-Protestant secularism, that is, it rests upon the foundations of a society which for a long time has officially relegated dogmatic religion to private life, while permitting a vague religiosity to pervade the public square. Protestantism became largely hollowed out theologically in the first half of the twentieth century, and the elites of our society, including journalists, have lost the superficial religiosity that was so common in the 1950s. But that religiosity had little content or significance. To quote Christopher Dawson once more,

> But at the same time the new forms of religion that were characteristic of America in the early days of the 19th century had little direct influence on the new American civilization which was being built up then. They represented an extremely individualistic type of Protestantism that was concerned, above all, with the individual conscience and the private experience of religious conversion....
>
> Thus American religion was detached from the objective world which was the domain of business and politics and focused on the subjective world

of religious feeling—above all the intense experience of religious conversion. This, I believe, has left a permanent mark on the American mind, so that, as several Americans have remarked to me, they find some difficulty in relating the two concepts of religion and civilization since these seem to belong to two quite distinct orders of existence. And hence the problem of the secularization of culture has not really been felt as an urgent one, since the two worlds of private religion and public social order do not touch one another.... [2]

Such an understanding of religion is not likely to attract people interested in the kinds of problems that affect civilizations, political or social problems, for example. So it was easy to throw off such a religious garment, since it meant little in the first place. Of course, this understanding of religion is entirely foreign to Catholic thought or tradition, but Catholic thought and tradition have had little impact on American social life. As the Catholic convert and Columbia University history professor, Carlton J. H. Hayes, said in an address to the Catholic Women's National Convention in December, 1921, "Nevertheless, in spite of the Church's amazing growth, American Catholics have had no such influence upon the thought and life of the whole nation as their numbers would lead us to expect."[3] The United States is a thoroughly Protestant country, or now, post-Protestant, and the sooner Catholics realize that, the better. For this fact must be determinative of how we undertake our apostolates here, not in the sense that the Americanists of the nineteenth

---

[2] "America and the Secularization of Modern Culture," B. K. Smith Lecture in History, under the auspices of the History Department, University of Saint Thomas, Houston, 1960.
[3] "A Call for Intellectual Leaders," reprinted in *The Catholic Mind*, vol. 20, no. 14, July 22, 1922, pp. 261–75.

century wanted, but in the sense that we must know what sort of cultural milieu we are dealing with. Just as St. Paul preached differently to the Athenian philosophers and to observant Jews, so we must realize the sort of audience we are trying to reach. I stress, however, that this does not mean that in any sense we water down the Faith or omit the "hard sayings" that are part of our doctrine, but that we realize how odd an integral understanding of Catholicism must seem to someone raised in the peculiar American milieu.

Moreover, we must make special efforts to guard our own minds against the influences of this post-Protestant culture, for unfortunately, even in the best days of the Church in the United States, there was little awareness of the fact that we needed to make efforts not only to convert individuals and families to the Faith, but to convert American culture, to make it Catholic, and this often in ways that were not obvious, that went beyond the legitimate but narrow concerns of the Legion of Decency, say. American preoccupation with moneymaking, with freedom, American rejection of authority, both ecclesiastical and social—these were only some of the cultural deformities that Catholics needed to address, but most often were either overlooked or, worse yet, it was believed they could somehow be given a Catholic veneer, incorporated into a Catholic way of life.

Can you be more specific about this question of the conversion of culture? How did Catholics fail to convert the culture in the United States? Were there opportunities to actually change the culture?

Well, they failed mostly in not trying, or not even understanding the need for a conversion on that level. Certainly there were figures who saw some of the problems with aspects of American culture, but what was lacking was a full-scale effort directed toward the conversion of our culture. In too many cases Catholics were all too eager to claim that we were better Americans than the Protestants, or at least that we could be. This was to let ourselves be Protestantized, culturally speaking.

Were their opportunities to convert the culture? Probably not any that were likely to succeed, but I don't think we looked for opportunities either. For example, we could have tried to make our convert-making activity also an opportunity for cultural catechesis. I acknowledge that that would have difficult in the age when the idea of the "melting pot" was all the rage. Probably had we tried to do so, we would have been labeled as subversives. It was German-American Catholics who grasped the cultural issue more than most immigrants, and established a large network of periodicals, organizations, and so on, to provide a counterculture to Protestant America. But this German cultural network was largely destroyed, for the most part, it is true, after the U. S. entered World War I on the side of the allies, but that wasn't the only source of friction at the time. American Protestant advocacy of Prohibition, for example, which naturally Germans and notably German brewers opposed, was another source of conflict that pitted a Catholic way of life against American Protestantism.

How can a man born in an environment where natural truths are so obscured or outright denied, come to a knowledge and acceptance of supernatural faith, which in many instances presupposes such truths (e.g., existence of God, permanency of marriage between a man and woman, objectivity of truth, to name a few)?

It seems that your question is really about how we might convert people to the Catholic faith today. I wish I had an easy answer to that, but I don't. When I read conversion stories, e.g., from the Coming Home Network, a significant number are of former Protestants. If Protestants are able to break away from their unthinking assumption that the Bible is the source of all Christian truth, then very often they can come to see the fact that it was a Church which Jesus Christ established, and that that Church is simply the Catholic Church. But how to get non-religious people, people who know little about the natural truths you mention, about philosophy, even about history, I do not know. I can't speak about Europe or Latin America, but in the U. S. the Church is hardly even on many people's mental maps, that is, they are unaware of her rich intellectual and cultural tradition and that that tradition has anything of importance to contribute on any subject at all. Insofar as they even think of the Church, they frequently lump her in with the most anti-intellectual and absurd forms of Protestantism or their views are shaped by the horrible clerical scandals of recent years. If the latter is all people know about the Church there is little wonder that they hardly give her the time of day.

And of course, there is the whole postmodern ambience, which has many ramifications which are hardly favorable to acceptance of Catholicism, or even to a consideration of its truth claims, or to any real truth claims at all.

Perhaps right now we should be concentrating our efforts more on keeping Catholics in the Church. As everyone who pays attention knows, the Church has suffered huge losses in recent decades. Now there are many reasons for this fact. In Europe and Latin America this has occurred too, and certainly the unfortunate and sometimes confusing direction the Church has often taken since the Council is in great part responsible. But not entirely. Here in the U. S. the Church has always had large numbers of defections, and I'd bet that if everyone who on arriving in the United States as a Catholic had remained so, together with all his descendants after him, we would have a majority Catholic population right now. In any case, one would hope that it would be easier to evangelize those who are already members of the Church, and it's certainly a place to start. But even to retain significant numbers of young Catholics will require a thorough-going reform of our institutions, our schools and parishes in particular. Many of them really don't have much of a Catholic commitment or a Catholic ethos. So if those who run and staff these institutions are pretty much victims of contemporary thinking, we've first got to help them to see what's wrong and to change. That there are no easy answers here should be clear to everybody.

It seems that in today's increasingly charged and polarized world simply stating some fundamental truths which previous generations would have never questioned makes those who state such truths isolated from the rest of society. How does a Catholic remain steadfast and resist the temptation to despair?

To resist the temptation to despair requires virtues, primarily the virtue of faith, by which we believe all that the Church teaches. In view of the difficulties you cite, plus the unhealthy state of the Church, we all need this virtue more than ever to remain steadfast. I think the greater potential problem is Catholics losing their faith on account of the perceived weakness of the Church and the hostility of the world. I mentioned this already, the absolute necessity for us to make our identity as Catholics our primary identity. Not our identity as citizens of a particular country, nor as conservatives or liberals — in fact, we should eschew those labels — but as Catholics. Only then do we have some hope of remaining faithful, including faithful in our thinking. And of course, the greater the number of Catholics who do so, the larger the community of the true faithful there will be — something which will make it easier for us to resist temptations to despair or to abandon the Faith.

What do you think Catholics should be most aware of in these politically and ecclesiastically charged times?

In a way it's the same things that Catholics should always be aware of: adherence to the Faith, keeping close to our Lord in prayer and the sacraments. But the way this plays out in different times is not always exactly the same. Right now we need to try to keep our balance, intellectually above all, because if our thinking is off balance, everything else will be. The late Jesuit, Father John Hardon wrote, "All the evil in the world begins with error. Or, more personally, all sin in the human heart begins as untruth in the human mind."[4] There's a tendency, perhaps most exaggerated in the United States, to look on sin solely as a moral question, to separate goodness from being, to forget not only that sin begins in untruth, but that ultimately sins are absurdities, attempts on our part to reorder the natural and divine order that God created. One can even say that in the end, every sin violates the principle of non-contradiction. As C. S. Lewis said of Milton, "We know from his prose works that he believed everything detestable to be, in the long run, also ridiculous; and mere Christianity commits every Christian to believing that 'the Devil is (in the long run) an ass.'"[5] For example, things like transgenderism, are evils, but they're evils first and foremost because they are absurdities. This is very important, for otherwise we segregate morality into some realm apart from being, from reality, and hence in much modern philosophy ethics is a problem because of this disconnect from reality, from being. So we need to keep our thinking clear. How can we accomplish that? One very

---

4 *Spiritual Life in the Modern World* (Boston: St. Paul Editions, c. 1982), p. 36.
5 "Satan," from *A Preface to Paradise Lost* in Arthur E. Barker, ed., *Milton: Modern Essays in Criticism* (London: Oxford University Press, c. 1965), p. 197.

important thing is to read books that help form our thinking, to stay away more from social media, for example, which offer the very antithesis of clear thinking.

Everyone should, as much as possible, ground his thinking in good philosophy and theology, making sure that he reads old material as much as new. And as I said before, read widely in the writers of the Catholic intellectual revival. They were close enough to our time that their concerns are understandable to us, and so they generally will give us a truly Catholic way of looking at our own contemporary situation.

While the list can be seemingly endless, could you give the readers a list of about 10 books, classic or contemporary, which can help them begin or strengthen them in developing a robust Catholic vision of life? And in connection with this, why is reading good literature important? How would one even define 'good literature'?

Books can help form a Catholic vision of life in many different ways — by teaching us about Catholic history, by forming a Catholic outlook or approach to reality, and so on. So the following is my very subjective list.

I'll begin with Hilaire Belloc, usually seen primarily as an historian. And I would not by any means downplay his historical works, which are always interesting and thought-provoking. But I have found his works of social and cultural criticism even more valuable, for example his book, *Essays of a Catholic*, an interesting and varied collection. "The Two Cultures of the West," which I already mentioned, is truly a must read. Then a little known book of his, *An Essay on the Nature of Contemporary England*, will give a concrete example of Belloc's sociological method applied to the England of his day. But pretty much anything by Belloc is worth reading.

When we think of Belloc, Chesterton immediately comes to mind. His variety and fecundity lead, I suppose, to everyone having his own favorites. Probably mine are *Orthodoxy*, *St. Thomas Aquinas*, and *The Everlasting Man*. But there are real gems to be found in all his collections of essays.

I tend to think of Christopher Dawson as the third member of the trio with Belloc and Chesterton. And also in his case I can highly recommend nearly anything. *The Dynamics of World History* is perhaps a good starting point, a collection of essays published in various periodicals and at various times.

When we turn to history, that is, to the history of social institutions, Richard Tawney's *Religion and the Rise of Capitalism*, which I mentioned as influential for me, will give a good sense of the medieval Catholic ethos as regards economics. In this same vein, Bede Jarrett's, *Social Theories of the Middle Ages, 1200-1500*.

Fulton Sheen's short book, *Justice and Charity*, originally a series of radio broadcasts from the late 1930s, will give readers a good sense of just how radical in their criticisms of the American economy orthodox Catholics were at the time, which ought to make us wonder what has happened. Why are we so complacent today, so willing to accept injustices with a shrug, or even to try to justify them with the aid of ideologies that are not consistent with a Catholic viewpoint?

Then, lastly, some might find my own book, *The Catholic Milieu*, helpful. In it I attempted to set forth what were the chief elements of a Catholic culture or a Catholic way of common or social life.

As to the second part of your question, much depends on what you mean here. By "good literature" do you mean what is often meant, novels, plays, and so on? I'd like to approach this question in another way, however. I mentioned above Fr. Antonin Sertillanges, the French Dominican, and his important book, *The Intellectual Life*. At the very beginning he distinguishes between two approaches to study and the intellectual life. He writes,

> Everyone has the duty to work; and after a first early and toilsome training no one acts wisely if he lets his mind fall gradually back into its primitive ignorance; but the effortless maintenance of what one has acquired is one thing, and it is quite another to consolidate from the foundations upwards a sum of knowledge recognized as merely provisional, seen to be simply and solely a starting-point.

Too often those who receive the rudiments of a liberal education, say, as an undergraduate, make little or no effort to maintain that. They seldom read serious books after graduation and see no reason why they should. They've gotten their degrees and probably some sort of technical training, which perhaps has enabled them to have a successful career. That is all they ever wanted. It's remarkable that discussions of the value of a college degree in the U. S. always focus, usually exclusively, on the so-called *return on investment,* whether someone will probably get back his monetary investment, what he has paid out for his education. For example, put "college return on investment" or even "college value" into a search engine, and you're likely to come up with an article such as this, "College Tuition vs. Investing: Is It Worth It?" The writer begins,

> With the cost of college rising each year and questionable career prospects awaiting college graduates, some people are wondering if a college education is still worth it. If you took all of the money you would spend on a college degree and invested it, would you come out ahead? Are college loans worth it?[6]

---

6   https://www.investopedia.com/articles/personal-finance/062515/college-tuition-vs-investing-it-worth-it.asp

Nothing here about the value of forming one's mind, about becoming a more aware participant in our cultural heritage or even a better citizen, and so forth. So Americans are probably most in need of hearing Sertillanges when he says that "no one acts wisely if he lets his mind fall gradually back into its primitive ignorance." And this is doubly so today and for Catholics in particular, for we face huge challenges that are at bottom intellectual challenges, both within the Church and outside her, in the world. If we don't understand the forces arrayed against us, if we treat something as merely a political question, or even simply as a spiritual or moral question, we really don't understand it very well, for at the root of these questions are differing ideas, differing understandings of reality. Sadly though, Catholics are no more likely to see beyond the cash value of higher education than others. Anyone who thinks that the Catholic mind in America has not been thoroughly colonized by our Protestant intellectual environment should simply read the following:

> A Georgetown University study has shown that Catholic colleges and universities provide a strong return on investment (ROI) and an unparalleled value.
>
> Analysis by the Association of Catholic Colleges and Universities (ACCU) of data published by the Georgetown University Center on Education and the Workforce (CEW) found that students who graduate from Catholic institutions earn a higher ROI than their peers in nearly any other sector, particularly over the long term.[7]

Earlier I quoted Father John Hardon that "All the evil in the world begins with error. Or, more personally, all sin in

---

7 https://manhattan.edu/news/archive/2020/10/study-shows-catholic-colleges-provided-unmatched-return.php

the human heart begins as untruth in the human mind." This point can hardly be overemphasized. Too many Catholics simply limit themselves to noting that something is wrong, not to the underlying fact of the error involved. For example, talking about the contemporary nonsense of sex-change operations, or as they're now called, "gender affirming surgery," our first reaction should be to say: *This is nonsense. This is absurd.* For the wrongness or evil of something is based on some error. Evil, remember, is a lack, a lack of the being that is due to some particular thing. And unless we recognize the ontological evil that precedes moral evil, then we'll never be able either to understand or to effectively oppose such evils.

The contemporary world is very complex, intellectually speaking, and hard to navigate. We need to have enough of a grasp of intellectual principles, of philosophy and history, especially, to be able to make sense of the contemporary situation, the world in which God has placed us. If we can't perceive the erroneous ideas upon which moral evils are based, not only can't we successfully argue against them, but we're in danger of being taken in by them without realizing it. We should strive to be at home in the world of ideas so that we can understand what is being said, why, and what its implications are, and how it all measures up against the twin standards of faith and reason. I like what G. K. Chesterton wrote about this.

> Ideas are dangerous, but the man to whom they are least dangerous is the man of ideas. He is acquainted with ideas, and moves among them like a lion-tamer. Ideas are dangerous, but the man to whom they are most dangerous is the man of no ideas. The man of no ideas will find the first idea fly to his head like wine to the head of a teetotaller.[8]

---

8 *Heretics* (New York: Devin-Adair, 1950), p. 299.

Living as Catholics in the Modern World

Different people have different vocations and different opportunities and duties, certainly, but we should all do our best to maintain, and if possible, to increase, our intellectual understanding of the fundamental truths that underlie reality, of the world around us, of the chief ideas that govern our time and that affect the state of the Church and the world. One can hardly have any kind of apostolate to his contemporaries if he doesn't understand their perception of reality. Today such an understanding of reality and of the contemporary world is necessary just to be a good father or mother, for our children and grandchildren are encountering all sorts of insane ideas and we had better be able to say more than, *That's wrong*. We have to understand these errors, to understand why they are wrong. Note also, that there is no error without some measure of truth, however small. Thus we have to be able to offer a Catholic alternative that includes or provides for whatever element of truth the error itself contains, but at the same time is larger, more beautiful, and, of course, more in accord with the reality of human nature and the nature of all things.

Wide reading is usually the primary tool for doing this, and what books we choose depend in part on our interests and the place where God has placed us. Whether we read chiefly history or philosophy, social thought or novels — all these can be justified and no one should be too narrow in his reading, for, as I remarked before, most important questions transcend the boundaries of one intellectual discipline. Novels and plays can be very helpful for understanding how past ages actually lived and how the reigning intellectual ideas of the time affected everyday life. Sometimes an illustration from fiction or from a travel account, say, can help one to understand the application of an abstract idea more easily than pages of simple discussion. I remember the first time I went to Ireland, in 1983. At the time Ireland still retained a fundamentally Catholic culture, at least on an everyday level, and I felt I learned as much about how a Catholic culture actually lives the Faith from that trip than from pages of reading about Catholic cultures. Of course, this in no way means that I do not value abstract discussions of things — I hope that is clear from what I've already written. But often we can be helped by concrete illustrations, either read about or actually experienced in our lives.

A Guide To My Work:
THEMES AND RECOMMENDATIONS

I was received into the Catholic Church in early 1978 and began writing shortly thereafter, first occasionally and then regularly. Although I have written about many different matters, there is one fundamental theme which unifies most of what I have published: this is the theme of the external, public life and work of the Church of Jesus Christ and of her members, especially insofar as these members form what we can call a Catholic culture. That is to say, I have written little on theology proper, but much on the intersection between Catholic faith and life in this world, and more on the life of Catholics in community than on what characterizes or should characterize the life of an individual Catholic.

This common life of Catholics may be conveniently summed up in the phrase *Catholic culture*, a concept I discovered not too long after my conversion in the famous essay of Fr. George Bull, S. J., "The Function of the Catholic Graduate School" (originally published in *Thought* in 1938). Fr. Bull wrote,

> In recent years, Catholics have become increasingly conscious of the clash between Catholicism as a general culture, and the culture of the world around them. The work of men like Belloc, Maritain, Christopher Dawson and others, has shown that we differ not in religion alone, but in the whole realm of unspoken and spontaneous things, which color even our daily routine.

One could say that this concept has been at the root of most of what I have written over the past nearly 40 years.

Some of my earliest articles for *The Wanderer* and *Social Justice Review* discuss aspects of this theme, but I developed it most fully in my first book, *The Catholic Milieu* (Christendom Press, 1987), which treats systematically the features of a Catholic culture.

One of the topics discussed in chapter 4 of that book is the political ramifications of a Catholic culture, the political as understood in the classical sense of "the ordering of things in a state toward the common good," which is a necessary part of human affairs and of any culture. But after that book was published, partly as a result of becoming more aware of the controversy regarding the decree on religious liberty of the Second Vatican Council, *Dignitatis Humanae*, the document which, according to so many, does away with or reduces to nothing, the concept of an explicitly Catholic political regime, I felt the need to expand on the specifically political arrangements and institutions of a Catholic culture, for such a culture without a corresponding political order seemed to me vulnerable, and moreover usually lacking the freedom to encompass all aspects of social life. Thus my second book, *Foundations of a Catholic Political Order*, published in 1998, which treats specifically the nature and structure of a Catholic state, including an approach to harmonizing *Dignitatis Humanae* with earlier papal teaching. Even before the book appeared I put forward this approach to the religious liberty question in an article in *Homiletic & Pastoral Review*, later revised for the book itself.[1]

I have returned to this theme of the political more than once, however, for it became clear to me that man's need for a political structure had deeper roots even than protecting

---

[1] Still earlier I had published an article on *Dignitatis Humanae*, in the spring 1989 issue of *Faith and Reason*, "The Problem of Religious Liberty: a New Proposal," but this was a preliminary sketch which needed further development.

cultural goods. Man, after all, according to Aristotle and St. Thomas, is a *political* animal, that is, we are creatures created by God in such a way as to require not only society, but authority, a theme treated more fully in my essay "Government, Society and the Human Good" published online in December 2012 on *Anamnesisjournal.com,* though no longer available there. In this essay I also contrast the classical and Catholic understanding of society with that championed by John Locke and embodied so completely in the American polity. The recognition that not only does Catholic teaching and tradition support a certain understanding of politics and society, but that the United States has from the beginning embodied a very different approach to these matters led me to write more than once on this subject. My most extended essay on this is "John Locke, Liberal Totalitarianism, and the Trivialization of Religion," *Faith & Reason*, vol. 26, no. 3, autumn 2001, and I have since returned to this question in several online pieces published on *Ethika Politika*, most notably "The Revenge of Religious Liberty" (May 2013), "The Catholic Failure to Change America" (April 2014), and "What is the Christian Understanding of the Social Order?" (March 2015).[2]

Even before I became a Catholic I was aware of the robust tradition of Catholic social teaching from reading Richard Tawney's great work, *Religion and the Rise of Capitalism*. Afterwards I became aware of the papal social encyclicals, and began to discover their voluminous commentaries and related publications, including the distributist tradition of G. K. Chesterton and Hilaire Belloc. I have written considerably in defense of distributism and in criticism of capitalism and free-market economics. Here my most extensive discussions include "Capitalism and Distributism: Definitions and Contrasts," *Faith & Reason*, vol. 27, nos. 2/3/4, summer/autumn/

---

2 Some of these essays or articles were included in my book, *From Christendom to Americanism and Beyond* (Angelico Press, 2015).

winter 2002, "The Implications of Catholic Social Teaching for Economic Science," *The Catholic Social Science Review*, vol. 14, 2009, and "Is Usury Still a Sin?" *Communio, International Catholic Review*, vol. 36, no. 3, fall 2009. Numerous shorter pieces dealing with particular points of economics or Catholic social doctrine may be found in my online *Distributist Review* and *Practical Distributism* articles. Among these I would single out "The Starting Point for Economic Thought" (July 2011), "Economics and the Real World" (December 2011), "Too Few Capitalists or Too Much Capitalism?" (June 2012), "The Just Wage" (October 2012), "The Butcher, the Baker, the Candlestick Maker" (December 2012), "Aquinas on Buying and Selling" (May 2013), "Economic Efficiency and Human Good" (June 2013), "The Spirit of Capitalism" (July 2013), "The Profit Motive" (October 2013) and "*Laudato Si'* and the Critique of the Technocratic Paradigm" (May 2016), on the first website, and "Why Unemployment is a Pseudoproblem", (November and December 2016), on the second. I had a essay on distributism and agrarianism in the spring/summer 2018 *Chesterton Review*, entitled, "Distributism? — or, Three Acres and a Cow?" And in 2020 I wrote an extensive article on distributism in the form of an interview for the July/September issue of the Italian journal, *Bollettino di dottrina sociale della Chiesa*. The original English of this interview/article was published on the website *Practical Distributism* early in 2021.

In 1997 and 1998 I published in the journal, *The Catholic Faith*, a connected series of articles on the papal social encyclicals. These together with some other articles on Catholic social teaching were collected in the volume *An Economics of Justice and Charity* (Angelico Press, 2017).

Related to Catholic social teaching and to the socio-political stance which Catholics should adopt is the question of the labels used in our political and journalistic discourse, especially *conservative* and *liberal*. I believe that these labels as currently used in American political discourse correspond to no reasonable categories of political or social thought, and I have critiqued them in a number of articles, including "The Superficiality of 'Left' and 'Right,'" *New Oxford Review*, vol. 59, no. 8, October 1992, and more recently "Futurists and Conservatives," *Ethika Politika*, April 2015. But the term liberal does have a meaning and a place in political thinking, as long as it is used to denote the civilizational trend away from a Christian social order that began in the late Middle Ages. In the book already mentioned, *From Christendom to Americanism and Beyond*, I included an essay, "Liberalism's Three Assaults" (originally published in the *Homiletic & Pastoral Review*) which discusses liberalism in this sense, and more recently I translated and wrote an introduction for Louis Cardinal Billot's critique of liberalism (Arouca Press, 2019).

In the 1990s the question of the place of Western culture with relation to the critique made by multiculturalism, especially in education, began to receive considerable public discussion. This led to my third book, *Christendom and the West*, in which I discuss the related but by no means identical concepts of Christendom and of Western culture. It seemed to me that many Catholics were more interested in defending the post-Enlightenment West than historic Christendom, and that some of the features which they celebrated as essential factors in Western culture were in fact inimical to a Christian social order. Particularly in the second chapter of that book, "The West and the Vocation of Christian Civilization," I point out how Western culture is a secularized Christendom, although it retains some of the unique characteristics and tendencies that were contained in Christendom, such as the missionary spirit and a universalism that is a sad parody of the truly Catholic universalism of the Church and the culture that she created.

One of the features of modern Western culture that is often credited to our Catholic past is the scientific enterprise as carried on since the 16th century. I believe that this is a mistake, and that modern science, far from being based on Catholic and scholastic understandings of reason and nature, exhibits a partial and domineering attitude toward the natural world, based on the thought of such innovators as Bacon and Descartes. I have discussed aspects of this theme in a number of pieces, most notably in "Aristotle, Your Garden and Your Body," *Homiletic & Pastoral Review*, vol. 93, no. 5, February 1993, "Catholicism and the Natural World: A Commentary on the *Catechism of the Catholic Church*, Nos. 337-344 and 2415-2418," *The Catholic Faith*, vol. 5, no. 6, November/December 1999, and "Saving the Appearances? C. S. Lewis' Critique of Scientific Knowledge," *Sehnsucht: the C. S. Lewis Journal*, vol. 10, 2016. This question of the understanding of natural science has received far too little attention, I think, even by those thinkers who are concerned to combat the corrosive scientism of our time, for unfortunately too many Catholics and others have simply accepted the presentation and understanding that science makes of itself, and fail to subject that presentation to any significant critique. Related to this is the question of technology, which I treated of briefly in *The Catholic Milieu*, and later in "The Problem of Technology," *Caelum et Terra*, vol. 2, no. 1, winter 1992 and other articles. More recently I edited the volume, *The Glory of the Cosmos: a Catholic Approach to the Natural World* (Arouca Press, 2020), in which I along with seven other authors discuss aspects of this Catholic approach to the natural world.

From an interest in how societies or cultures embody different cultural or religious ideals I also began writing on two related themes, first on the historical trajectory of how the modern world became what it is, and secondly on the question of culture directly. On this first point see "The Dissolutions of Modernity and the Response of Thomism," *Doctor Angelicus, Annuarium Thomisticum Internationale*, vol. 4, 2004, "What is Western Culture? Three Examples, Three Disputes," *New Blackfriars*, vol. 89, issue 1019, January 2008, and several shorter pieces published on *Ethika Politika*, including "Reason, Traditionalism and the Enlightenment" (February 2012), "America and the Evangelization of Culture" (June 2012), "The Varieties of American Exceptionalism" (July 2012), "Natural Law, Politics, and the Transformation of America" (August 2012) and "The World, Modernity, and the Church" (March 2014). Some of these pieces, along with other contributions to the same subject, have been collected in my fourth book, *From Christendom to Americanism and Beyond*.

On the latter subject, culture, or more strictly, the philosophy of culture, I have published several papers, "Culture and the Embodiment of Cultural Ideals as Preliminary to a Philosophy of Culture," *Forum Philosophicum*, vol. 14, no. 1, spring 2009, "Human Nature, Human Cultures and the Communication of the Knowledge of God," *New Blackfriars*, vol. 95, issue 1059, September 2014, and "Nature and Culture as Human Spaces," *Studia Philosophica Estonica*, vol 8, no. 1, 2015 (online) and the chapter, "What Account can Philosophy give of Culture?" in the collective volume, *Prologue to Provocations: A Search for Truth in Christian Anthropology*, edited by Fr. Romero D'Souza (New Delhi: Christian World Imprints, 2016).

My most recent book, co-authored with John Médaille, *Theology: Mythos or Logos? A Dialogue on Faith, Reason, and History* (Angelico Press, 2020) is more directly philosophical or apologetic than most of my writings. In this book John and I deal with how the Catholic faith, and how coming to believe, is related to reason and to history.

As a writer I find myself returning again and again to the same themes, sometimes because of new thoughts or greater knowledge of the subject, sometimes because I feel the need to treat them from a slightly different standpoint. Similarly, changing currents of thought both in the Church and outside her have suggested topics to me, and often I have written in response to someone else's utterance, or to a polemic penned against some position of my own.

PRAISE FOR PREVIOUS WORKS

The Catholic Milieu

"We need more sobering assessments such as Storck's. I look forward to an extensive treatment of the subject by this author."
— Cuthbert Claxton in *Reflections*, fall 1989.

"... an incisive reminder of the insipidity of American culture."
— *New Oxford Review*, June 1989

Foundations of a Catholic Political Order

"... a timely and clearly argued account of what a Catholic state governed with traditional Catholic social teaching would look like..."
— Thaddeus J. Kosens in *Culture Wars*, April 1999

"Storck has written a book that bears witness to the maximizing demands of the Faith in relation to the world." — Peter A. Kwasniewski in *Homiletic & Pastoral Review*, November 1999

Christendom and the West

"But the first step in re-Westernizing and re-Catholicizing one's self and environment is to understand what one has lost and why one should attempt to regain it. In order to achieve this end, study is needed. Not surprisingly, I nominate Storck's *Foundations of a Catholic Political Order* and *Christendom and the West*."
— David Arias, Jr. in *New Oxford Review*, May 2000

From Christendom to American and Beyond

"Mr. Storck in the present volume illustrates the way in which the historian can emerge as a prophet, teaching us not only about the past but warning us of the abyss that we face in the future if the disastrous path we have been following is not abandoned. Like Belloc, Thomas Storck is not merely an historian but a prophet. He needs to be heard and heeded."
— Joseph Pearce in *The Distributist Review*, March 2016

"The book is filled with enormous eruditon and cogent analysis, not only of liberal modernity, but of the Christendom it replaced—that far more organic social order in which the Faith permeated everything..."
—Roger Buck, *Cor Jesu Sacratissimum*, February 2016

An Economics of Justice and Charity

"If you want to delve into the untapped treasure of the Church's social justice teaching, *An Economics of Justice & Charity* is the place to begin. Storck is an ideal guide to explore the papal magisterium on this subject."
—Shane Kapler on *Just a Catholic* blog

"A balanced and informative work, it rightly highlights a sometimes neglected aspect of Church teaching, and as such is worth the attention of any serious Catholic."
—Donal Anthony Foley in *Catholic Herald*, May 2018.

Theology: Mythos or Logos?

"John Médaille and Thomas Storck engage in a dignified debate about faith and reason which they frame in terms of *mythos* and *logos*. These two concepts, we learn, wind their way around human affairs in countless ways. The book takes the form of a series of letters that the two Catholic thinkers wrote to each other—letters in which an argument is developed that pulls the reader along in a way few philosophical books do."
—Michael De Sapio in *The Imaginative Conservative*, February 2021

"It is indeed an exemplary dialogue, earnest, hard-hitting, sophisticated, and wide-ranging, but always amicable. One almost forgets in an age of tweets and parleys that such a sustained high-level conversation is possible."
—Peter A. Kwasniewski on Amazon.com

www.ingramcontent.com/pod-product-compliance
Lightning Source LLC
Chambersburg PA
CBHW021426070526
44577CB00001B/79